Wooden figurehead from bow of whaler White Lady.

The Story of YANKEE WHALING

ILLUSTRATED WITH PAINTINGS, PRINTS, DRAWINGS AND PHOTOGRAPHS OF THE PERIOD

THE STORY OF

YANKEE WHALING

by the editors of
AMERICAN HERITAGE
The Magazine of History

narrative by IRWIN SHAPIRO
in consultation with
EDOUARD A. STACKPOLE
Curator, Mystic Seaport,
Marine Historical Association
Mystic, Connecticut

PUBLISHED BY
AMERICAN HERITAGE
PUBLISHING CO., INC.
NEW YORK

BOOK TRADE DISTRIBUTION BY
GOLDEN PRESS · NEW YORK

FOREWORD

NO OTHER INDUSTRY in America's history ever approached whaling for adventure and enterprise. From the early Colonial days when boat-crews attacked the whale near shore, through the development of deep-sea whaling by the hardy Quaker whalemen of Nantucket, and on into the adventure-packed century when Yankee whalemen made the world their domain, the real account of whaling is one in which free enterprise in all its essence was practiced to the fullest.

The factual narrative presented here brings young readers some of the flavor of this great industry, and tells the story of American whaling in terms more exciting than fiction could ever achieve. For history was never meant to be the dull record of the past. It should be nothing less than a dramatic re-staging of life itself.

The drama of those centuries, when the American whaleman made his country known in every remote part of the world, is recaptured here. The accounts of long-forgotten episodes and stories are as thrilling in this presentation as a reading between the lines of the unvarnished records assures us they must have been. For the understatement of those whalemen-adventurers (who, in their own journals, rarely exploited their accomplishments) seldom permitted them to supply details, even when relating far-flung adventures of the most heroic proportions.

But in this book, their stories are told for them in bold narrative style, with illustrations which make a perfect backdrop for the telling. The editors of American Heritage Junior Library have made every effort to guarantee authenticity. The text has been carefully checked; the old drawings, whalemen's sketches, period prints, paintings, and photographs, have been selected in an effort to set forth what is, virtually, a pictorial history of whaling. This accuracy in reporting, together with a colorful array of pictures, combine to make *The Story of Yankee Whaling* a book which cannot fail to stimulate the young reader's imagination.

EDOUARD A. STACKPOLE

LIBRARY OF CONGRESS CATALOGUE CARD NUMBER: 59-14690
 Designed by Artists and Writers Press, Inc. Printed in the U. S. A. by Western Printing and Lithographing Company. Published by American Heritage Publishing Co., Inc., 551 Fifth Avenue, New York 17, N. Y.

Long before American colonists went whaling, the Basques, the Dutch and the English hunted whales. This 1744 engraving shows English whalemen in Greenland.

CONTENTS

A right whale.

WHALE OFF!

Long before white men settled in America, there were whales in the sea—and there were Americans to catch them. These Americans were Indians. They had no ships and could not go hunting whales across the oceans of the world. Instead, they waited for the whales to come to them.

And the whales did come. In their majestic travels over the Atlantic, the great beasts swam near the shore to feed. Sometimes during a storm a dead whale would drift ashore, and the Indians would cut it up for the meat and bone and blubber. Sometimes a whale would wander into an inlet or bay, and the Indians would attack it from canoes.

Captain George Waymouth, an English explorer, saw Indians whaling off the coast of Maine in 1620. He wrote that they went after a whale "with a Multitude of their Boats; and strike him with a Bone made in fashion of a harping iron [harpoon] fastened to a rope; which they make great and strong of Bark of Trees, which they veer out after him; then all their Boats come about him as he riseth above Water, with their Arrows they shoot him to death; when they have killed him and dragged him to Shore, they call all their Chief Lords together and sing a Song of Joy. . . ."

Captain Waymouth forgot one thing in his report. Attached to the ropes of the harpoon were drogues—blocks of wood or blown-up bags made of skins. The drogues floated in the water and kept the whale from diving too deep or swimming too fast.

And the whale that Captain Waymouth saw killed must have been a small one, for a large whale could not be killed with arrows. The Indians surrounded a large whale, stabbing and jabbing it with lances. At last—if they were lucky—the whale died from loss of blood. But more often it swam out to sea and the Indians sadly watched it escape. In their light canoes they could chase it no farther.

When the English colonists settled on the northeast coast, they also waited for whales to come to them. At first they were satisfied with the dead whales that were cast up on the sandy beaches. Then, again like the Indians, they took to boats and went whaling along the shore. They soon improved on the Indians' methods. They built better boats, mostly of cedar. They made better harpoons and lances, with tips of iron instead of bone or stone. They gave up the use of drogues. They attached the rope of the harpoon to the boat itself, so that the whale was forced to tow his own enemy behind him.

Shore whaling was begun in the Massachusetts Bay Colony. Some of the settlers moved from Massachusetts to Long Island, and it was the Long Islanders who, in the 1640's, first made whaling a regular bus-

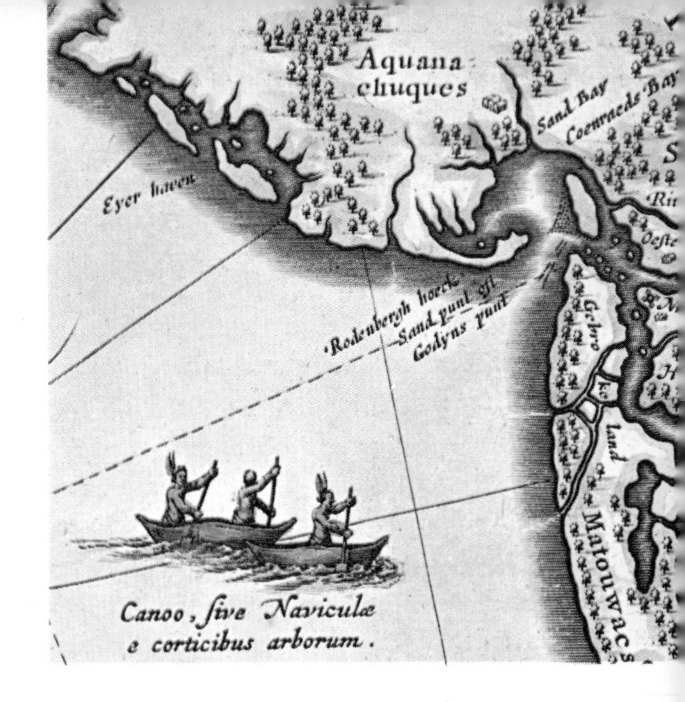

The detail above, from Blaeu's map of "New Netherlands and New England—1635," shows Indians using log canoes. In the picture below, taken from a world map drawn by a Frenchman, named Desceliers, in 1546, Indians are whaling in a canoe of the same type. The monster's mustache and forked tail suggest that the artist knew very little about whales.

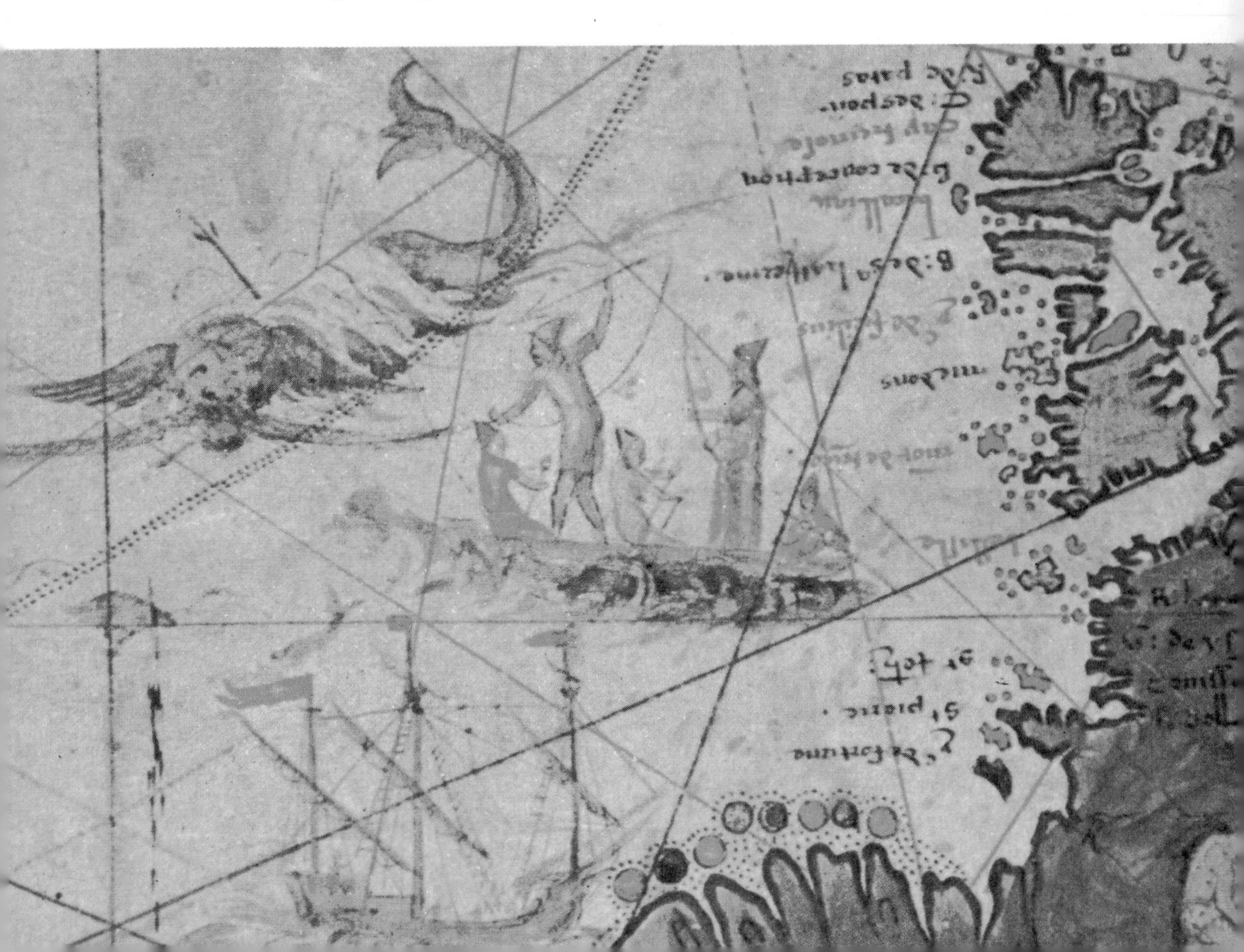

Off-shore whaling out of East Hampton and Southampton on Long Island is depicted in this "Map of Ye English Empire in Ye Continent of America," drawn around 1700.

iness. In East Hampton and Southampton they formed companies to hunt for whales. By 1650, using somewhat larger boats, they were making expeditions along the coast lasting two or three weeks. All day the crews searched for whales; at night they slept on shore.

From the beginning, lookouts were stationed along the beaches to keep watch. As soon as a lookout spied a whale, he sang out, "Whale off!" and ran up a signal flag on a tall mast. The men of the company would come running to the beach, board the boats in six-man crews, and go off after the whale.

Many of the lookouts and crewmen were Indians. Red man and white man worked side by side. The Indians were friendly, brave, experienced in whaling—and they worked for low wages. The companies were anxious to hire the skillful Indians, and the towns passed laws to keep their wages from going too high. In 1672 Francis Lovelace, the governor of New York, ordered that "whosoever shall Hire an Indyan to go a-whaling, shall not give him for his Hire above one . . . Cloath Coat, for each whale hee and his Company shall kill, or halfe the Blubber, without the Whale Bone, under a Penalty herein exprest. . . ."

After a whale was caught, it was hauled up on shore, and the bone and blubber were cut out. The blubber was "tried out"—boiled down to oil—in big iron try-pots. And, as the smoke rose from the blazing wood fires, over the neat towns floated the rich, ripe stink of boiling oil.

So powerful was the smell that Southampton passed a law about it: "Whereas the trying of oyle so near the street and houses, is soe extreme noysome to all passers by, especially to those not accustomed to the sent thereof, and is considered hurtful to the health of people, and is very dangerous (if oyle should fire) for firing houses or haystacks, the cort doth order that noe person after this present yeare shall try any oyle in this towne nearer than 25 poles from Main Street, under penalty of paying five pounds fine."

But to the whalemen it was a healthy smell, a good smell, a sweet smell. The world needed whale oil for lamps and candles, and they were bringing light from out of the dark depths of the sea. And whale oil meant money in their pockets.

In the early days of whaling, lookouts kept watch atop tall masts on shore.

In fact, on Long Island the oil itself was used as money, to pay debts and taxes. East Hampton paid its minister and its schoolmaster partly in oil.

Long Island whalemen cutting blubber from a whale. The men at left are sharpening cutting spades on a grindstone. One whale might yield over 100 barrels of oil.

GRAPHIC ILLUSTRATIONS OF

SHEWING THEIR UTILITY TO MAN, IN THEIR EMPLOYMENTS DU

For Light _ Sperm Oil & Candles.

Sperm Whale Fishery.

For Food.

Published by ROAKE & VARTY, 31, Strand, Londo

The Whalebone.

Agriculture _ For Manure.

Manufac

Published by ROAKE & VARTY, 31, Strand, London

Designed & Drawn on Stone by W. Hawkins

THE WHALE.

Uses of the whale are shown at left. Before 1859, when the first successful oil wells were drilled, whaling was an enormously important industry. Whale oil was used as fuel for lamps and as a lubricant for machinery; the waxy spermaceti was moulded into fine candles.

For the children of Long Island, whale oil had a special meaning. Schools were closed during the whaling season, which ran from December to April. The boys had to lend a hand, helping to catch whales or try out oil.

A faint whiff of whale oil even reached far-off London, where sat the king who ruled England and all its colonies in the New World. The king's government put a tax on oil and the Long Islanders refused to pay. They elected Samuel Mulford, the head of a whaling company, to the colony's Assembly. Time after time he was in trouble with the Royal Governor for fighting the tax. Twice, in 1704 and 1716, he left his home on Main Street in East Hampton and carried the fight to London.

The English looked curiously at the angry old man. They smiled at his old-fashioned clothes of homespun, and at his cane with its handle carved from a whale's tooth. They said that he had sewn fishhooks in his pockets to discourage pickpockets. But when he stood before the King's Council and spoke up for the colonists' rights as Englishmen, they listened. And in 1720, the new governor of New York reduced the tax on whaling.

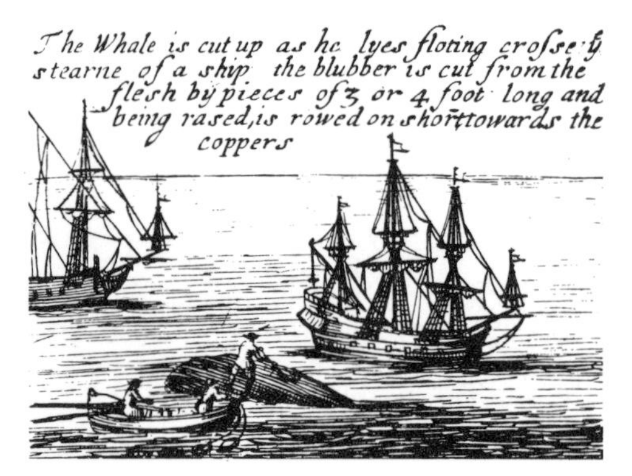

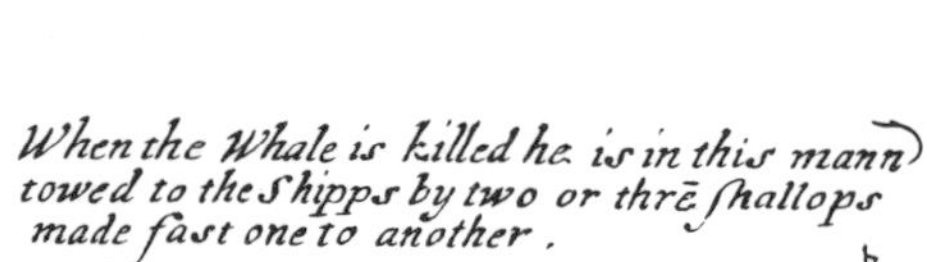

North of Long Island, in the colonies of New England, the try-pots were bubbling, too. There was shore whaling off Cape Cod and Nantucket, and some off Martha's Vineyard and Salem.

In 1672, the Nantucketers invited James Lopar of East Hampton to settle on Nantucket and teach them what he knew of whaling. He went to Nantucket, but for some reason decided not to remain, and the Nantucketers went on whaling in their own way. Around 1690 they made the same kind of invitation to Ichabod Paddock of Cape Cod. This time they got their teacher.

Nantucket was a small island, and early in its whaling days the south side was divided into four equal parts. Six men were put in charge of each part. Five of them stayed in a small hut, while the sixth climbed to the top of a mast and kept a lookout for whales. When he sighted one, he sang out or blew a horn, and the six men would launch a boat and row after the whale. There were

The seven small engravings show whaling off Greenland in the 17th Century, much as it was done later off the shore of New England. The right whale (center) has no teeth. It strains its food through the baleen, the hundreds of plates of whalebone growing from the roof of its mouth. Whalebone, used for whiphandles and stays in corsets and hoopskirts, was also found in other baleen whales, such as the humpback.

often Indians among the crew. They received a share—or a "lay," as the Nantucketers called it—of the oil and bone.

Like the other off-shore whalers, the Nantucketers hunted the kind of whale called the right whale. It was given this name simply because it was said to be the right whale to catch. It had no teeth and it was mild, for a whale. It swam close to shore and floated after it was killed.

Peleg Folger, a whaleman of Nantucket, once described the right whale as "very large, hollowing on the back, all slick and smooth, having no hump at all as other Whales. The bone (of which is made stays and hoop'd petticoats) doth grow in their mouth. The tongue is monstrous large and will commonly make a tone of oyl. He has two spout holes and makes a forked spout whereby he is distinguished from other Whales at a distance."

But there were other kinds of whales in the sea, as Nantucketers found out. Around 1700, a sperma-

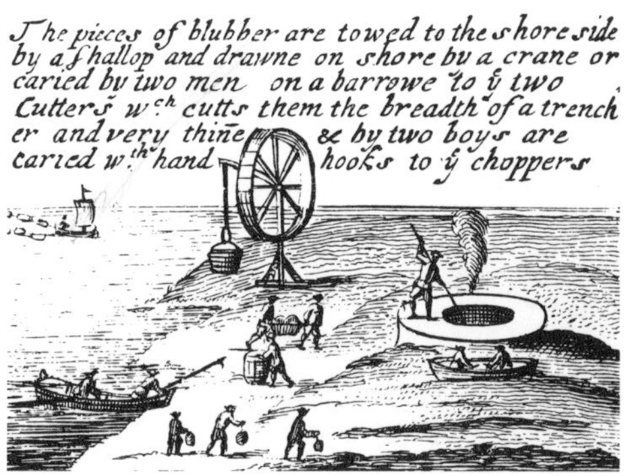

After a whale was harpooned, it often gave whalemen a speedy "Nantucket sleigh ride."

ceti, or sperm whale, was cast up dead on the shore. It was larger than the right whale, and its blubber made a better oil. It had a large hollow in its head filled with pure oil and spermaceti, a sort of wax that was excellent for candles.

Peleg Folger wrote that the sperm whale "will make from 10 to 100 barrels of oyl. He has no bone in his head and his brains is all oyl. He has a hooking hump on the after part of his back one spout hole, and his under jaw is full of ivory teeth and his tongue is very small."

The sperm whale was a fighter. With its giant's teeth, enormous jaw, and mighty flukes, or tail, it was dangerous to men in small boats. But it loved deep water and steered its huge body away from shore. And so the sperm whale and the Nantucket whaleman seldom met—until the early 1700's.

Sometime around 1712, Captain Christopher Hussey and his crew

A sperm whale turns on its hunters.

went whaling in a small sloop. There was nothing unusual about that. They had gone whaling many times before, and always in a small sloop. For hours they cruised, going so far that Nantucket was out of sight, but they could find no whales. There was nothing unusual about that, either.

At last they decided to give up and return home. Suddenly, as they brought the boat about, a fierce wind came roaring down on them from the north. The waves rose high, breaking across the bow, and they were carried farther and farther out to sea.

And then, through the flying spray, over the heaving waves, they saw something, bulging darkly against the dark sky—a school of whales. One whale dived, and its glistening, squared-off hump came up again near the boat.

"Whale off!" cried the man in the bow.

The whale spouted. The spout was not forked like the familiar right whale's, but bushy, and it arched forward as it fell.

Captain Hussey muttered in surprise. "Be that a sperm whale?" he said.

A moment before, the bony hand of death seemed to be reaching for him and his crew. Now the wind still tore at their faces, the waves still pounded at the boat, the water still sloshed around their ankles—but they forgot all that and stared at the strange spout of the whale.

They were alive; and if alive, they had to earn a living. And they were Yankees of New England, where earning a living was hard. There was oil in that whale, and oil was money. And they were whalemen. They had come to catch a whale, and by thunder, they would.

Captain Hussey shouted an order, and the men no longer felt tired. From the sloop they launched a boat. They bent to the oars, and they battled the whale until there was a lance in its back and it turned over, dead.

Whales would fight to protect their young. Here a cow whale tries to rescue her calf.

But they had the storm to battle, too. The wind was roaring worse than ever, dumping so much water into the boat that they could not bail it out fast enough. Captain Hussey exchanged a few words with his men. Instead of battling the storm, they would retreat.

Quickly they rowed to the other side of the whale, which was away from the wind. Here the oil oozing from the carcass calmed the waves. Sheltered by the huge body of the animal they had killed, they waited out the storm.

After the storm was over, they towed the whale to shore. They were not disappointed. The whale they had killed was a spermaceti, and its oil was worth more than that of the right whale. News of the catch spread over Nantucket. It was important news, because right whales were already becoming harder to

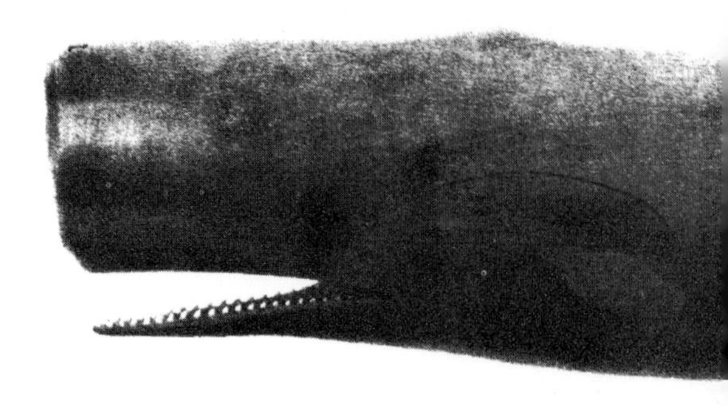

find. Nantucketers had always believed that sperm whales were rare, but it seemed that they were plentiful, farther out at sea. Captain Hussey had found a whole school of them, and had proved that they could be caught. Why should they bother with right whales when the sperm whales brought in more money?

Within a few years, Captain Hussey's neighbors were setting off in sloops—single-masted sailing vessels—on longer and longer voyages. Whalemen were going farther and

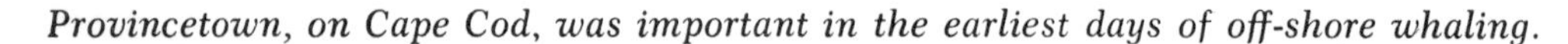

Provincetown, on Cape Cod, was important in the earliest days of off-shore whaling.

The huge sperm whale is a meat eater, who feeds on squid, tearing them apart with the teeth in his 25-foot jaw.

farther out on what the captains, in their writings, called "ye deep." The small island of Nantucket, itself like a large whale stranded in the shallows, was linked with the sperm whale, itself like a small island floating in the sea.

The great hunt for whales was on. It was a hunt that would take the whaleman among hot flowery lands swimming in golden air, with smiling girls and eaters of human flesh. It would take him among lands frozen under snow, with ice mountains lifting to skies cold as a fish eye. It would make him a wanderer on strange waters, half the world away from home, searching, searching, everlastingly searching for whales.

"The Birth of the Whaling Industry," by William Wall, shows whalemen trading with Indians in New Bedford. The sloop was the earliest sailing vessel used in whaling.

SHIP, MASTER, AND MEN

Thomas Nye, Jr. (above), a whaling captain of New Bedford, was painted in 1800. The painting (below) shows a 19th Century whaler fitting out in New London.

"What are you here for?" the captain said to the crew.

He might have been the captain of any whaler in the great days of whaling, and the crew might have been any crew. It was the custom then for the captain to make a little speech soon after the start of the voyage. Each captain had his own manner of speaking, but the meaning was always the same. He was the ruler of the ship; the crew's duty was to work and obey.

"What are you here for? Maybe some of you don't know, so I'll tell you. You come to go a-whaling—to get oil—to work. Work! That's what you're here for. We didn't ship you to play. If you've got any other idea, you'll find out your mistake. I'll see to that, I will.

"And I want to warn you—I'll have no fighting aboard my ship. Any quarrels you have, bring 'em to me. I'll settle 'em for you, I will. And I don't want to hear no swearing. It's an infernal bad habit, and I won't have it. If I catch anybody swearing, I'll see that he's flogged—damme if I don't.

"As for grub, you'll get plenty of vittles—if you work. If you don't work, there's a good chance you'll starve. No need to grumble about the grub, neither. If you don't get enough, tell me about it.

"Obey the officers' orders at all times. Do your duty, and I'll treat you well. But if you make trouble, look out! I'm not the man to stand for it, I ain't. No, not me. And don't you forget it.

"Well, the sooner we get a cargo of oil, the sooner we'll get home. I guess that's all. Now go forward, where you belong."

What are you here for? The words seemed to hang in the air, floating on the wind that pushed against the sails and hissed through the rigging. *Whales . . . oil . . . work* . . . . Not that any real whaleman needed to be told the answer. He could find it merely by glancing at the ship. Even a landlubber could

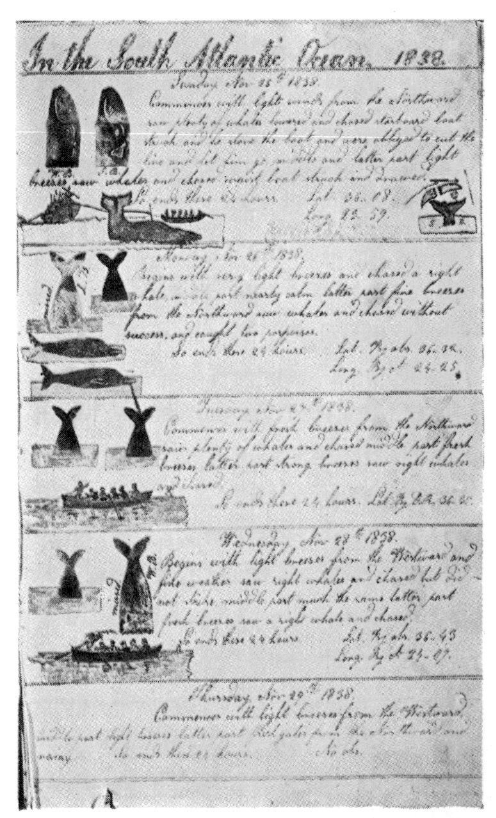
In the South Atlantic Ocean. 1838.

Sunday Nov 25th 1838.

So ends these 24 hours. Lat. 36. 08. Long. 23. 59.

Monday Nov 26th 1838.

So ends these 24 hours. Lat. By obs. 36. 32. Long. By ct 24. 25.

Tuesday Nov 27th 1838.

Wednesday Nov 28th 1838.

Thursday Nov 29th 1838.

In this page from a whaler's logbook pictures indicate both whales that escaped and those that were captured.

see the difference between a whaler and a merchant vessel—and between a whaleman and a merchant seaman.

For the seaman went to sea only to reach land. His trade was moving passengers and cargo. The sea was his highway, and he traveled it as swiftly as he could.

But the whaleman's trade was hunting, and the sea was his hunting grounds. He was a stranger to the land. His voyages lasted as long as four years, and the ship was his real home. It was also the base from which he hunted, his transportation, his storehouse and his factory.

He hurried his ship only when sailing to the waters where whales gathered, or when bound for his home port with a load of oil. Otherwise he cruised about slowly, keeping a lookout for whales. So the whaler did not have the graceful lines of the faster merchant vessels. She was built for work, not speed. Her hull was made of the strongest timbers. She was bulky, and broad in the beam, to hold oil and supplies and tools of the whaleman's trade.

Outfitting a ship for a long whaling voyage was a big task in itself. Extra food and water could sometimes be picked up in foreign ports, but everything else had to be carried on board. Just for running the ship and general housekeeping, there were such things as charts and compasses, frying pans and coffee pots, needles, nails, spare sails, medicines and meats. Then there were supplies for the slop

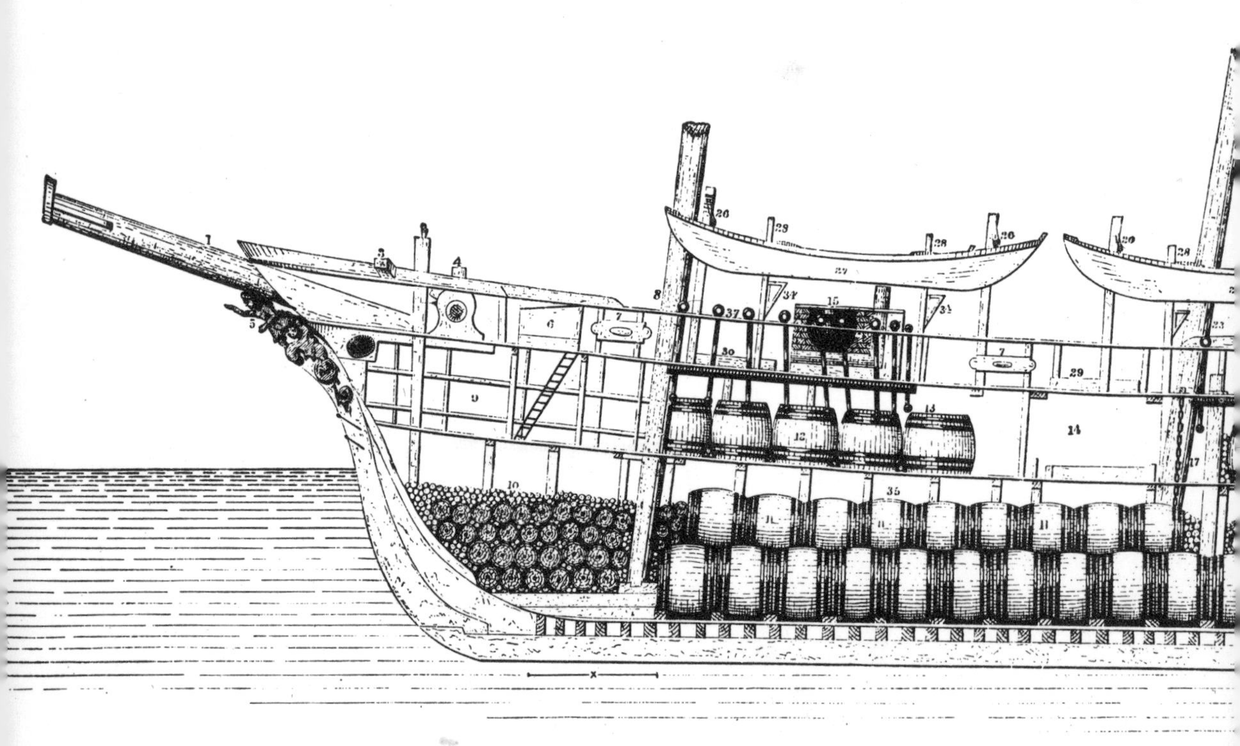

chest, a kind of store where the men could buy jackets, pants, hats, shoes and other articles for themselves.

The actual hunting was still done from open boats, as it had been in shore whaling. But now these boats, called whaleboats, were carried to sea on the ship. With them went their craft, such as harpoons and lances, and their gear, such as oars and coils of rope.

After a whale was captured, it was cut up and the blubber boiled. The ship became a factory producing oil. So factory equipment, too, went to sea. The try-works, a brick structure to hold the fires for boiling blubber, took up part of the deck. And in the hold were cutting instruments, try-pots, barrels to hold the oil, and staves to make more barrels. Altogether, thousands of different things had to be stowed aboard before a whaler could sail.

With so much of the ship used as a storehouse, little space was left for the men. The captain was the exception. He had a stateroom, where he slept, and a cabin with a desk and a sofa. On a few ships, his bed was a real luxury. It was hung from gimbals, a device that allowed it to swing freely. No matter how the ship tossed and rolled, the bed remained level.

The captain was truly the master of the ship and all on board. He could give orders to any of his men —and punish those who disobeyed. He received the best quarters and the highest pay. But his job was not an easy one. He was responsible to the owners for a ship and equipment worth from thirty to sixty thousand dollars. He had to know seamanship and navigation. He took care of all the ship's business, doctored the sick, settled arguments. He governed from twenty-five to forty-five men sailing strange waters for several years. Most important of all, he had to capture whales and bring home a "full ship"—a ship loaded down with oil.

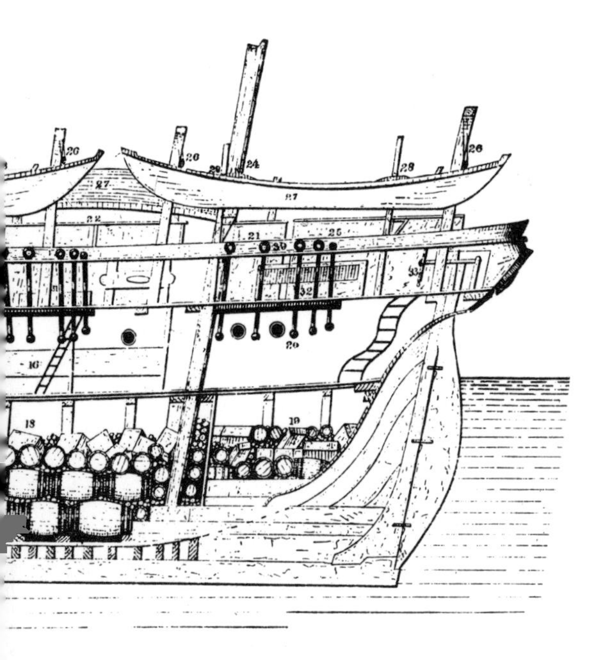

A cutaway view of the whaling bark Alice Knowles *of New Bedford shows whaleboats hanging from davits on deck, casks of whale oil stowed in the hold, the forecastle in the bow of the ship, and the captain's cabin in the stern.*

The ship-rigged whaler Niger *of New Bedford, painted in 1874 by Benjamin Russell.*

Next in rank were the officers—the first, second and third mates. Larger ships carried a fourth as well. The mates were in charge of the whaleboats when they were lowered over the side to chase whales. They were also in charge of the deck and supervised the crew. The first mate was second in command to the captain, and kept an eye on everything and everybody aboard ship.

The mates had staterooms opening off the main or forward cabin, which adjoined the captain's cabin. Like the rest of the crew, they slept in ordinary bunks. But they ate in the main cabin with the captain, and were served by a steward.

At mealtimes the captain always sat down at the table first. Then the mates entered the cabin, one by one, in the order of their rank. They left in reverse order. The third mate was the last to be served and the

Bark: square-rigged foremast and mainmast; fore-and-aft rigged mizzenmast.

first to leave. He did not dare to keep the others waiting after they had finished eating. If he did not gulp down his dinner in a hurry, he left the table hungry.

The officers' quarters were in the stern of the ship. Midship was the steerage, the quarters of the more skilled members of the crew. On one side was a stateroom for the harpooners, who were also called the boatsteerers. On the other side of the steerage was another stateroom, for the cooper, who made and repaired barrels, the blacksmith, the carpenter, the steward, and the cook. They ranked higher than the rest of the crew, and on some ships the harpooners ate in the main cabin, after the captain and the mates had left.

In the forward part of the ship, jammed between the bows, was a room shaped roughly like a triangle. That was the forecastle, the quarters for the foremast hands—the ordinary members of the crew. The walls were lined with narrow double-decker bunks. The only seats were the men's own sea chests, which were placed around the room, in front of the lower bunks.

As many as twenty men slept and ate in the forecastle. When the weather was bad, they came here to rest and smoke their pipes, to spin yarns and sing songs. Air and light could enter only through the hatch, which opened to the deck above. Crowded with them under the low deck beams were the smells of sweat and tobacco smoke, of wet clothing and boots, oil and blubber, and the dinners of a hundred yesterdays. And often, especially in the tropics, the men shared their small space with troops of insects.

At mealtimes the cook would call out, and several of the foremast hands would hurry to the galley. They picked up wooden or tin tubs, called kids, filled with meat, potatoes and vegetables, and a bucket of tea or coffee. They carried the kids to the deck or forecastle, according to the weather, and the other men came rushing up with their tin plates and cups.

The officers were served the best meals. The harpooners were served the same food, except for butter and sugar. They and the rest of the crew sweetened their tea or coffee with molasses. Molasses was cheaper. But officers, harpooners and foremast

The fore-and-aft rig of the whaler J. Truman *shows that she was a schooner.*

Two-masted topsail schooner

hands all ate a great deal of "salt horse" or "salt junk." This was heavily salted beef, something like corned beef. It had to be soaked in water for hours to make it ready for cooking.

Besides salt horse, whalemen ate pork, beans, rice, potatoes and codfish. Once or twice a week, for a treat, the cook made lobscouse, a hash of salt meat and hard bread. An even better treat was plum duff, a kind of pudding made of flour, lard, yeast, water and dried fruits. Sometimes, when a ship visited a port, there would be fresh meat, vegetables, fruit and water for a while. Live chickens and pigs were sometimes taken aboard and carried in crates on deck. This was the best treat of all, for as a voyage dragged on, the ship's bread became mouldy, the meat became rotten, and the water in the casks stank.

Three-masted schooner

Immediately after the beginning of a voyage, even though the ship was only on its way to the whaling grounds, lookouts were ordered up on the mast. The crew was divided into two watches, each headed by a mate. The watches took turns working—on duty four hours, off duty four hours—with two "dog-watches" of two hours each. It was just after the watches were chosen that the captain made his little speech. *You know what you're here for . . . whales . . . oil . . . work. . . .*

At first the men did the sort of work usual on any sailing vessel, and prepared for the whaling to come. The harpoons and the cutting instruments were carefully sharpened. The whaleboats were repaired. In good weather the "green hands" —newcomers to whaling—practiced handling the whaleboats.

Brig

The two dogwatches, from four to six and from six to eight o'clock in the evening, were the time for rest and relaxation. All hands came out on deck. They talked, they smoked their pipes, they read, they told stories of their adventures, they

Ship

patched their clothes. Led by a whaleman with a good voice, they sang songs like this one:

Our captain stood upon the deck,
A spyglass in his hand,
A-viewing of those gallant whales,
That blowed at every strand.
"Get your tubs in your boats, my boys,
And by your braces stand,
And we'll have one of those gallant whales,
Hand, boys, over hand!
So be cheery, my lads! Let your hearts never fail
While the bold harpooner is a-striking of the whale.

Sometimes they danced, and sometimes they "skylarked"—wrestled and scuffled and frolicked about. But, more than anything else, they scrimshawed.

Bark

Scrimshawing was carving and decorating the teeth and pieces of jawbone of whales. Whalemen made all sorts of scrimshaw to give as presents to their wives, sweethearts, or friends. They made rolling pins, clothespins, chessmen, dominoes, rings, bracelets, canes, penholders, footscrapers, doorknobs, yarn winders. They made thousands of jagging wheels, which were devices for crimping the edges of pie crust. There was not a whaleman's wife in Nantucket or New Bedford who did not own at least one.

Brigantine

Scrimshawing took time. And, once his ship had reached the whaling grounds, time was something every whaleman had a great plenty of. At night he stood only one watch of three or four hours. In the morning, before breakfast, he did a few small jobs, such as setting sail and washing the deck. During the day, he put in two hours steering or acting as lookout. But his chief duty was to capture whales.

Silhouettes show types of whalers. Ship, brig and bark were most commonly used.

Each whaling merchant had his own flag, often carrying his initial, to identify the various ships he owned. This chart, published in 1837, lists a hundred whaling merchants of New Bedford and the names of their vessels.

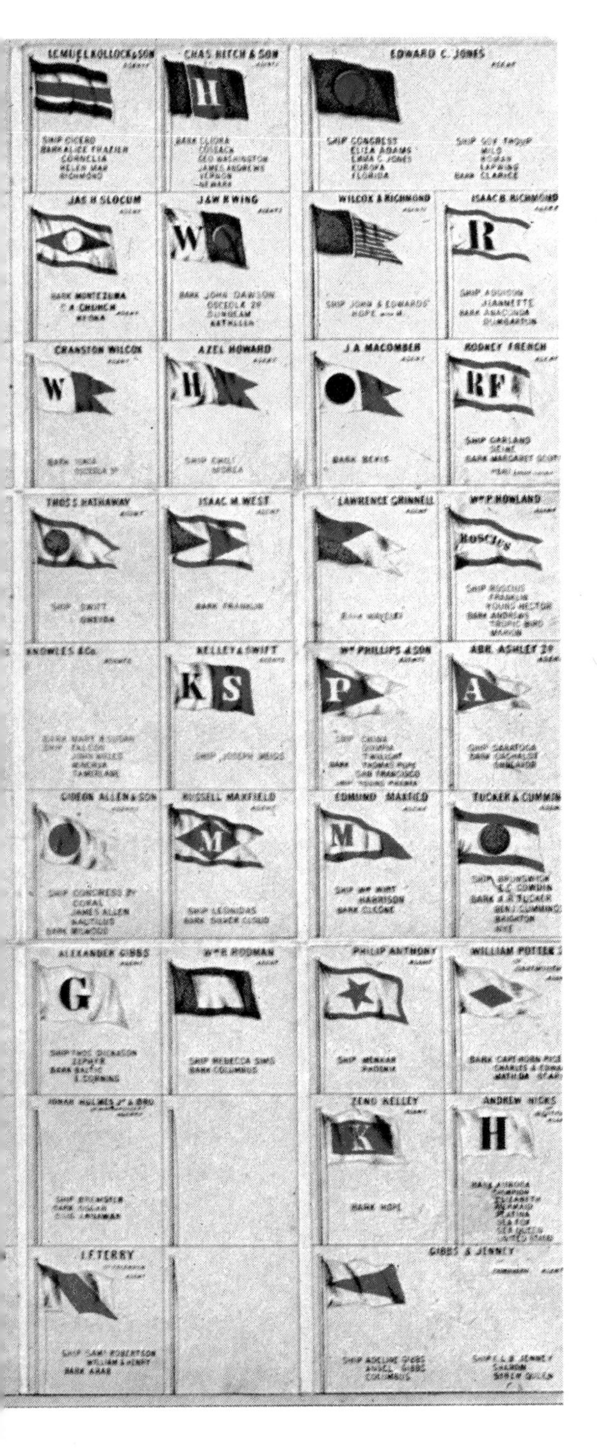

When whales were sighted, there was a stretch of hard, bitter, dangerous, bone-breaking work. Between whales there were long, empty hours with little to do but wait—and scrimshaw.

The story of those empty hours was told in some of the logbooks, or records, kept of each voyage by the first mate. The log of the *Acushnet*, for example, carried these notes:

"Sunday, Oct. 26, 1845—Your humble servant employ'd in killing time . . . December 16, 1845—Busy Doing nothing—nothing to do it with . . . Friday, January 23, 1846—Doing nothing special. Dull as you please . . . February 4, 1846—Calculated to see whales, made a miscallculation . . . July 4, 1846—Employed Eating & Drinking, fretting, Playing Backgammon & sleeping Mending a pair of pants. . . ."

One of the few breaks in a long voyage came when two whaling vessels met at sea. If the captains were friendly, they would hold a "gam." The captain and some of the crew of one ship would set out in a boat and visit the second ship. Meanwhile, the mate and some of the crew of the second ship would visit the first ship. The men exchanged news, gossip, yarns, books and newspapers. The cooks dished out plum duff to all hands. A gam lasted from a day to a week. Then the two ships separated, and the long, empty hours began again.

What are you here for? Whales, oil, and work . . . And to wait for whales, and scrimshaw, and watch the never-ending waves of the sea.

Whalemen enjoying a frolic on a gam.

In the early days of deep-sea whaling, the men who did the waiting were Yankees from Massachusetts and Long Island, from Nantucket, Martha's Vineyard, Cape Cod and Sag Harbor. There were also some Gay Head Indians, and some Negroes. Often all the men in a ship's crew were neighbors. Whaling was a career, and many a young fellow went to sea as a forecastle hand and in time worked his way up to captain.

But later, when New Bedford became the whaling center of the world, more men were needed. Captains and owners did not care where they came from. Half of a crew might be Americans; the rest would be of a dozen different races and nations. Yankees still went whaling, but fewer of them shipped out as forecastle hands more than once. The voyages were too long, the work too hard, the dangers too many, the living conditions too poor, the punishments too cruel—and the pay too low.

No whaleman was ever paid wages. Instead, he received a share of the profits of the voyage, called a "lay." A captain's lay might be 1/8; a cabin boy's 1/250. An ordinary forecastle hand's lay was from 1/160 to 1/100. All crew members were charged for clothes and other articles they bought from the slop chest. When this money was taken off the lay, a forecastle hand might end a four-year voyage with less than a hundred dollars in his pocket. Sometimes he even owed the ship money. A bright New England lad could do better at home, or he could go west and try to make his fortune.

And so, after 1835, most crews were young and green, with as many foreigners as Americans. Such crews were not easy to manage, and captains and officers often gave them

A whaler's crew, in the forecastle.

rough treatment. Mates were quick to use their fists, or the toe of their heavy boots. Captains punished their men by having them locked up or flogged. Not until 1850 did Congress pass a law that stopped flogging aboard whalers and merchant ships. Many men deserted when their ship made a foreign port, and more than one crew rose against its officers in a bloody mutiny.

Why, then, did any man go whaling? A captain went because he had a respected position, and a successful voyage filled his pockets with money. A poor Portuguese fisherman might go because to him the low pay was far more than he could earn in his own country. A homeless, jobless man might go because he could find nothing else to do. A green farm boy might go because the ship could carry him to adventure on the other side of the world.

What are you here for? Whales . . . oil . . . work. . . . And waiting, and loneliness, and scrimshaw, and wormy meat, and stinking water, and the curses of the mate. . . . The storms, the cold, the shrieking wind. . . . The terrible moment when the jaw of a whale rose dripping from the waves, and a stove boat, and broken bones, and maybe death in the dark sea. . . .

But sometimes, in the delicious warmth of the southern islands, among the strange tribesmen and the smiling girls, there was joy such as landlubbers could only dream of. And always there was the awful excitement of the chase, and the pride of the hunter who had fought and captured the mightiest creature on earth. It was the pride of conquering death itself, and it made even a homeless, beaten, ignorant forecastle hand know that he was a man.

This etching, made in 1846, shows the crew scrambling for "salt junk" at mess time.

A DEAD WHALE OR A STOVE BOAT

Driven by the hunger in their huge bellies, whales roamed the world. The bowhead, the humpback, and the right whale searched for brit—the vast masses of tiny, shrimp-like sea animals that floated

near the surface of the water. The sperm whale was even more of a traveler. It swam great distances seeking the giant squid, which it swallowed in chunks half the size of a whaleboat. And wherever whales went, hungry for brit or squid, there went the whalemen, hungry for oil.

But before the whales could be killed, they had to be "raised," or found. Every day, from sunrise to sunset, on every ship cruising the whaling grounds, a lookout was on watch at the masthead. Each foremast hand took his turn, staying aloft for two hours. The orders were always: "Keep your weather eye open, and sing out every time."

When lookouts on the masthead sighted a whale (above), boats were lowered and the chase (below) got under way.

Robert E. Weir, a whaleman on the bark Clara Bell, *drew these sketches for his journal. When two harpoons entered the "gallied" or frightened whale, it "sounded" or dived deep. Then, as it surfaced for air, the boatsteerer killed it with a long lance.*

Going on the Whale

The lookout stood on the top-gallant crosstrees, which were two narrow pieces of lumber nailed to the mast. His only support was a pair of iron hoops at the height of his breast. Perched a hundred feet above deck, in fair weather or foul, he watched miles of sea for signs of whales. The most common sign was the spout, the plume of vapor caused by the whale's breath.

As soon as he saw a spout, the lookout sang out, "There she blows! Blo-o-ows! She blows!" If he saw a whale leaping up from the water, he added, "There she breaches!" Or, if the whale was falling back on the water with a foamy splash: "There she white-waters!"

"Where away?" the captain would call from the deck.

The lookout's reply would give the direction of the whale, such as "Three points off the starboard

Gallied Whale Sounding

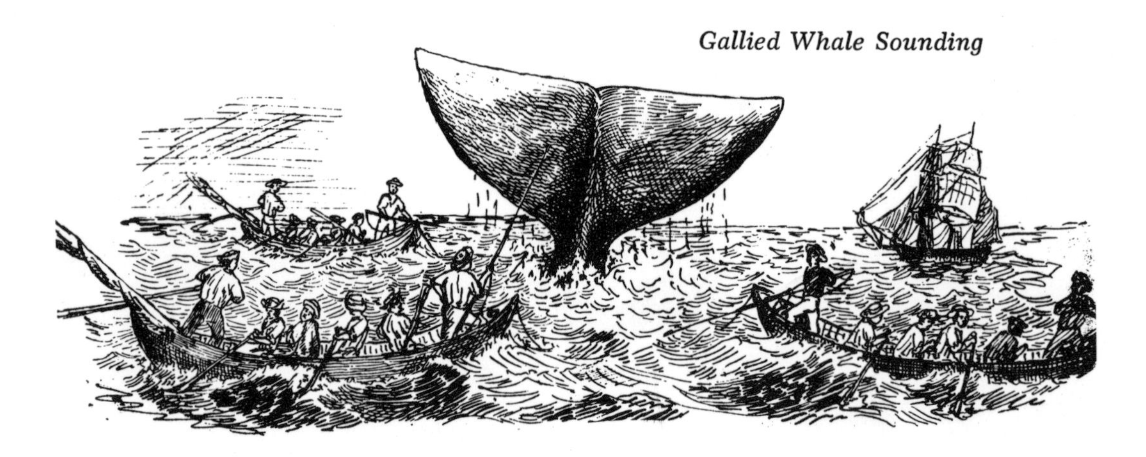

Darting the Second Iron

bow," or "Two points off the lee beam."

"How far?"

"Mile and a half, sir."

"Call all hands! Stand by to lower!"

At the captain's command, the ship seemed to shake itself and wake from sleep. The men came scrambling down the rigging and bursting from the forecastle. While the mates shouted orders, they ran to the whaleboats, their feet thudding on the deck. For this was the real business of whaling; this was what the whalemen were here for—to kill whales and get oil.

The whaleboats were ready. Light but strong, they hung from davits, a sort of crane used on ships. The men placed aboard them two wooden tubs in which were coiled about 1800 feet of line. Stowed aboard were harpoons and lances,

(Continued on page 42)

Reaching His Life

BENJAMIN RUSSELL'S WHALING PANORAMA

Long before the invention of moving pictures, both children and grown-ups were entertained by moving panoramas. These were paintings hundreds of feet long, unwound on two rollers so that audiences could see them from beginning to end. While the painting unrolled from scene to scene, it was explained by a lecturer who stood beside it on the stage of a public hall or theater. Sometimes it was also accompanied by piano music. Panoramas of the Mississippi River were especially popular.

*On December 5, 1848, a New Bedford newspaper announced: "*THE PANORAMA OF A WHALING VOYAGE AROUND THE WORLD*—Messrs. Purrington & Russell respectfully give notice that their great painting of a* WHALING VOYAGE AROUND THE WORLD*, now being completed, will be exhibited in a few days at* SEAR'S HALL*."*

The Russell mentioned in the announcement was Benjamin Russell, a member of

one of New Bedford's leading families. The Russells owned many whalers and merchant ships and much property, but during the hard times of 1832 and 1833 they lost their fortune. In 1841, at the age of 37, Benjamin Russell shipped out on the whaler Kutusoff. *At sea he began painting whaling scenes. After his return to New Bedford, he and an artist named Purrington began work on the panorama.*

Eight and a half feet high and 1,275 feet long, it was based on Russell's voyage on the Kutusoff. *It depicted various vivid whaling scenes, such as the one above which shows the capture of right whales in the North Pacific. The panorama was shown many times in New Bedford and in Boston, Cincinnati, Louisville, St. Louis, Baltimore and New York. It did not make Russell's fortune, but he went on painting, becoming the most famous of all whaling artists by the time he died in 1885. In 1911 the panorama was given to the Old Dartmouth Historical Society and Whaling Museum of New Bedford, where it is now preserved. Many pictures from that panorama are reproduced here.*

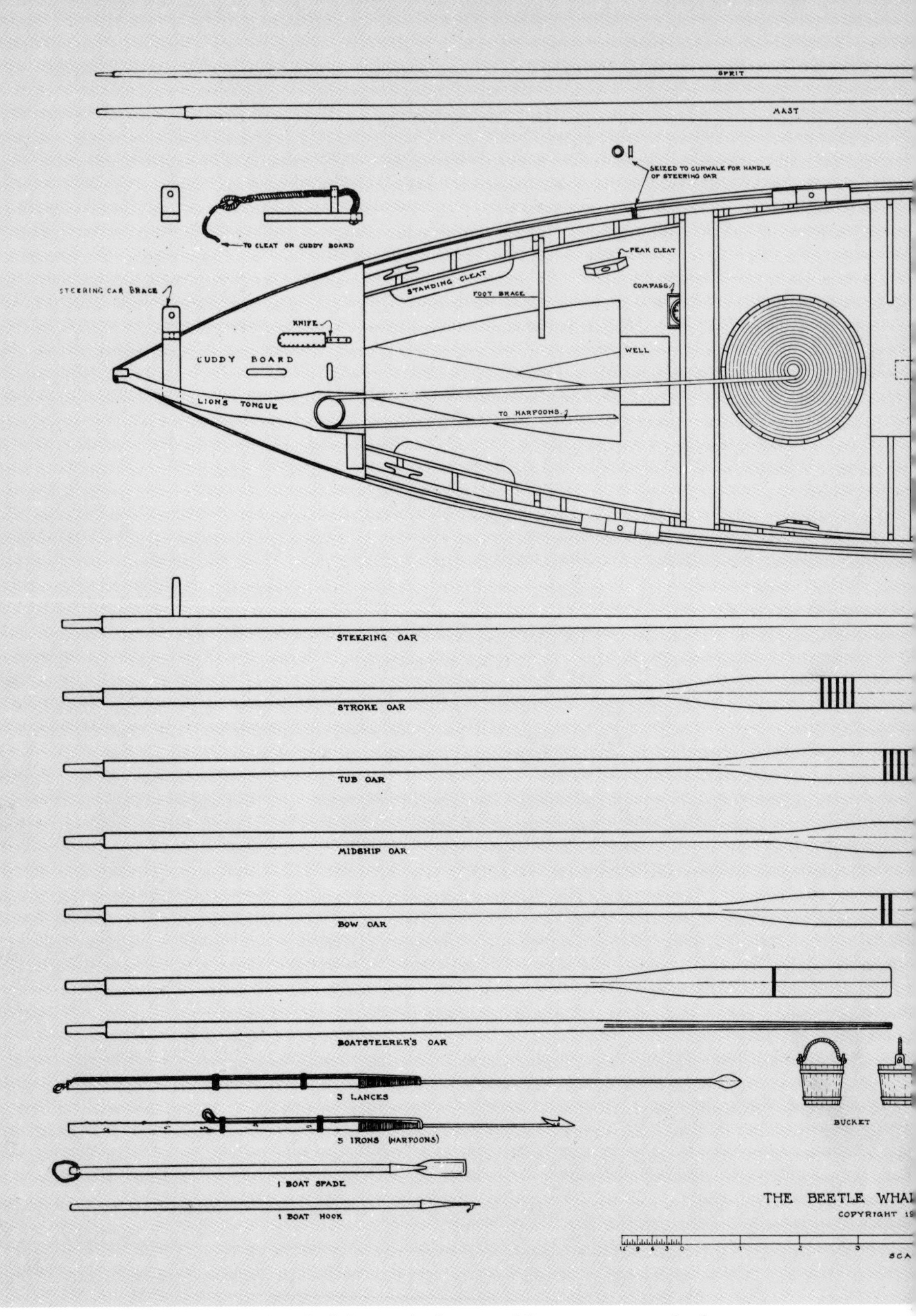

Scale drawing of a whaleboat, which carried five oarsmen and a boatsteerer.

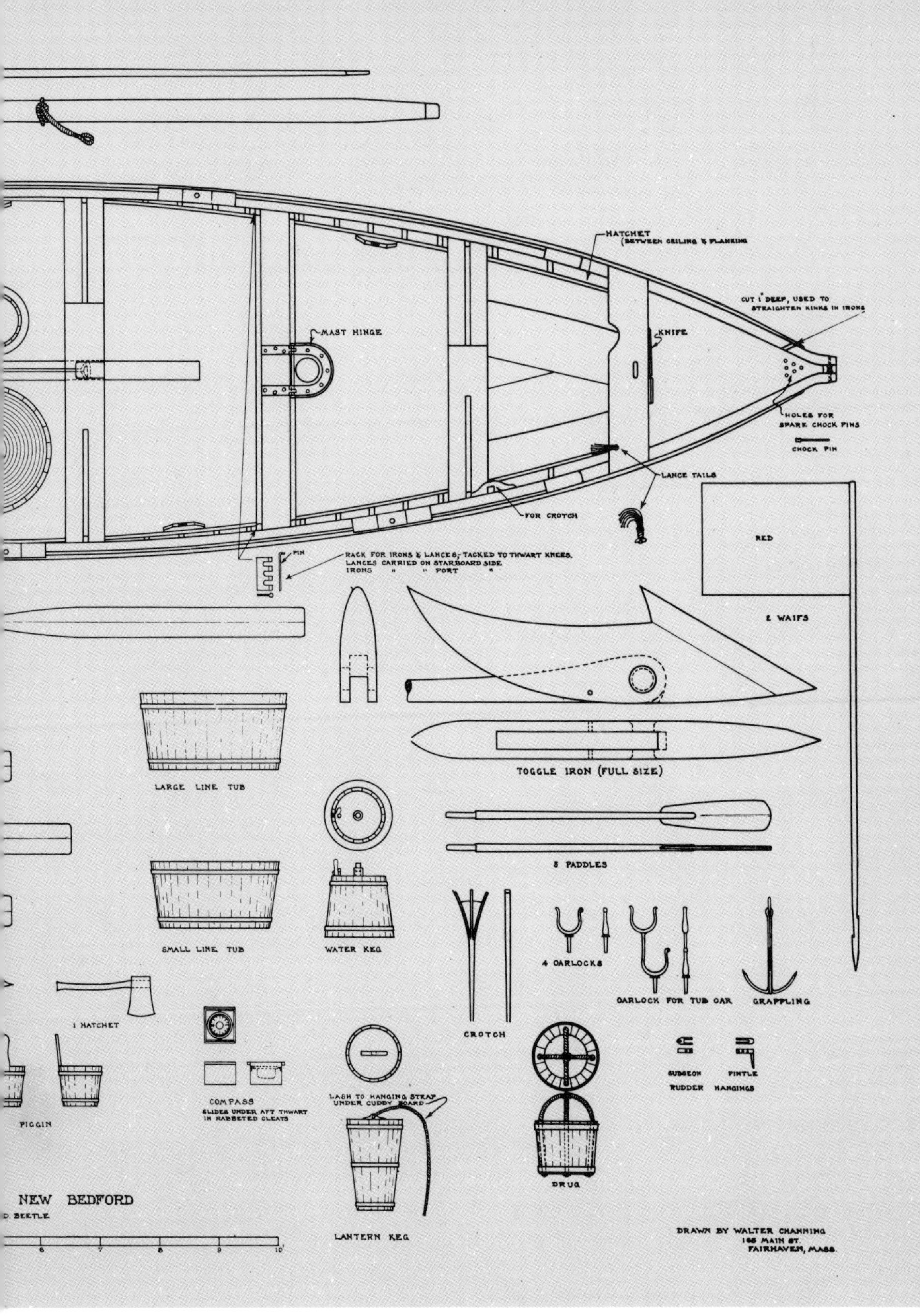

The harpooner set his knee in the notch in the bow thwart (right) as he threw his iron.

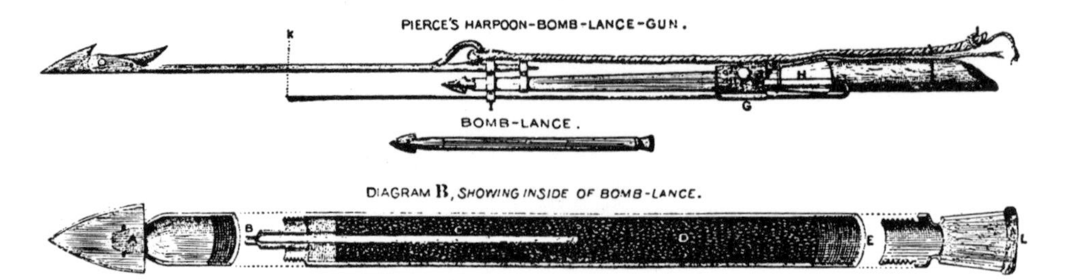

The harpoon gun, invented in 1856, fired a bomb which exploded inside the whale.

cutting spades, paddles, oars, a steering oar, a rudder, and a mast and sail that could be quickly set up or taken down. There were also a wooden bucket for bailing, a compass, and hard bread and water for emergencies.

Most whalers carried three or four boats. Each boat had a crew of six men, with the captain or a mate acting as headsman. "Lower away!" the captain ordered, and they lowered the boats into the water. Then, climbing over the rail and down the side of the ship, they leaped into the boats.

The headsman stood on a small platform in the stern, handling the steering oar and commanding the craft. The other men rowed. The harpooner, who was also called the boatsteerer, pulled the bow oar. The ship itself was left in the care of the shipkeepers, a small group of men, often headed by the cooper.

Sometimes, when the wind was right, the crews of the whaleboats raised their sails. Sometimes, to keep

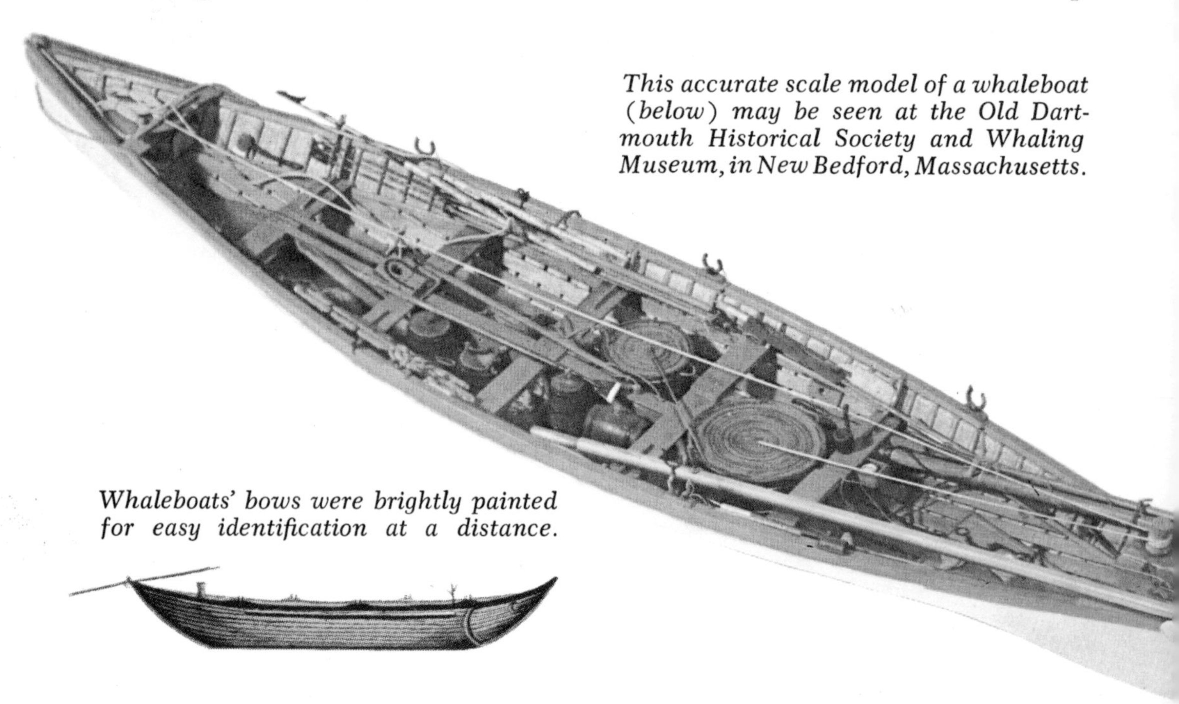

This accurate scale model of a whaleboat (below) may be seen at the Old Dartmouth Historical Society and Whaling Museum, in New Bedford, Massachusetts.

Whaleboats' bows were brightly painted for easy identification at a distance.

from "galleying" or frightening a nearby whale, they paddled their boats like canoes. But usually they rowed.

As the actual chase began, a wild excitement ran through the men. If killing whales was their business, it was also their sport—a rare, grand, and magnificent sport. Now they could forget the waiting and watching, the dreariness, the loneliness, the hardship. They would know these things again, of course, and soon. But during the chase they were more than sailors. They were kingly hunters, pursuing a monstrous beast over the rolling hills of the sea.

Part of the sport was racing the other boats. The crews fought to reach the whale first, even though with every stroke of the oars they pulled themselves closer to danger. It was a danger they could not see, for they rowed facing the stern. Only the headsman faced forward. Steering toward the whale, he would speak to his crew, shouting, roaring, swearing, joking, coaxing, commanding.

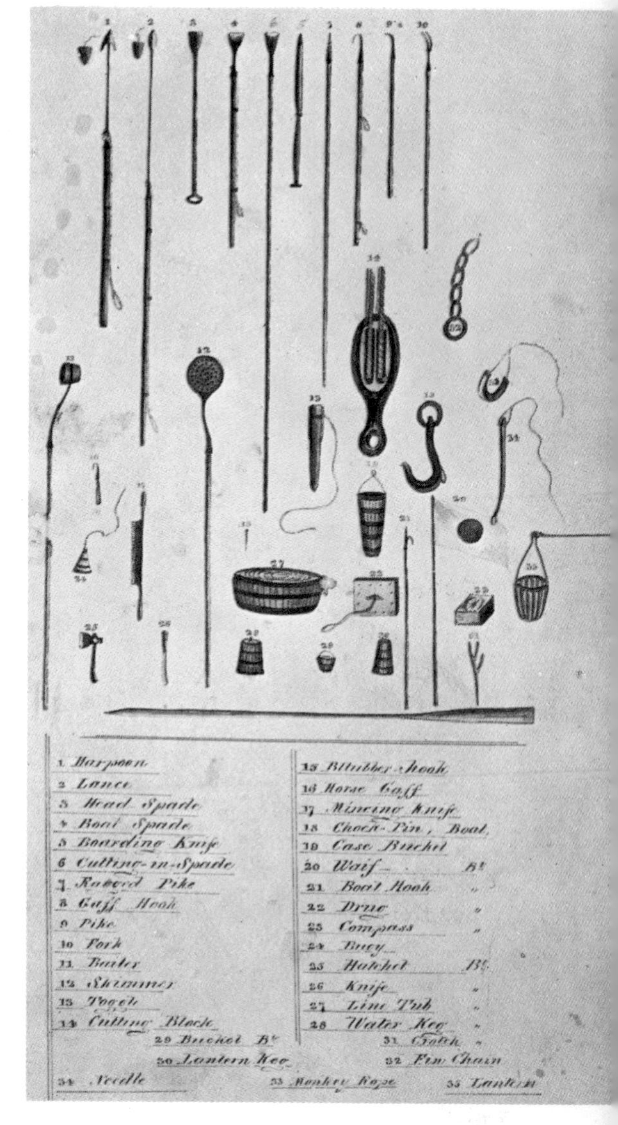

Implements used in whaling.

"Give way, lads! Give way! A long, steady pull does it. Pull, I say! Don't let those other boats beat ye! Pull like vengeance! That's it, that's it! We're gaining! Pull, every mother's son of ye! Crack your backbones! Burst your hearts and your liver and your lungs! But pull! Merrily, merrily! Yes, we're gaining! We're gaining! I tell ye that whale is ours! Shall we take it? Aye! A dead whale or a stove boat! Give way, my heroes, my hearties! Put

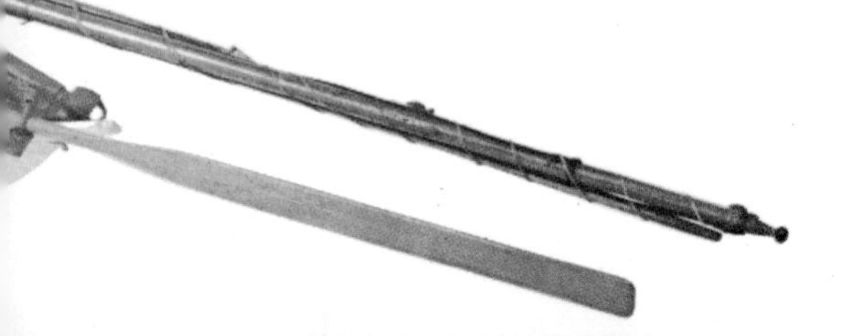

The crew strained at the winch, as a strip of whale blubber was hauled aboard ship.

your backs into it, ye rascals! Plum duff for supper if ye catch me that whale! Duff, did I say! I'll give ye tobacco! I'll give ye rum! Why, lads, I'll give ye anything I have! I'll give ye my house, I'll give ye my dear wife and children, if only ye pull! Thunder and lightning! Don't give up now, blast ye! Lay on, lay on! Are ye awake or asleep! Look alive! Smash your oars, double 'em up! Oh, if ye could see that whale, maties, you'd pull till your eyes popped like buttons! She blows! She blows! And there she white-waters! Softly now! Steady, steady . . . . Easy, lads, easy. There! There! Harpooner! Stand up! Stand by your iron!"

Rushing toward the unknown terror behind him, a green hand might go crazy with fear. He might jump

Sperm oil of the highest grade was bailed from the tank or "case" in the whale's head.

The "junk," or blubber, was first carved into blocks, called "horse pieces."

over the side, to be hauled back to life by one of the boats, or to drown before anyone could reach him.

Meanwhile the harpooner balanced himself on the small platform in the bow. In his hand was a harpoon, a line attached to the blunt end.

"Give it to him!" said the headsman, when the boat was within a few feet of the whale.

And the harpooner darted the harpoon, which struck deep into the monster.

"Give him another iron!"

And the harpooner flung a second harpoon.

"Stern all! Stern all, for your lives!" the headsman shouted, ordering the crew to back the boat away from the thrashing whale.

(*Continued on page 48*)

"Horse pieces" further sliced up as "Bible leaves" were then boiled in the try-pots.

The try works, where blubber was boiled, or "tried out," stood on deck, behind the mainmast. Crew skimmed off the hot oil as it collected, and barrelled it after it had completely cooled.

Fed with scraps of blubber, the fires of the whaleships' try works glowed late into the night, until every drop of oil was stowed below in the cooling tank.

At right are two pages from the log book of the whaler Mary and Susan. *On the left-hand page are the signals used on the voyage, and a record of the whales which were sighted but got away; the right-hand page lists the whales which were captured and the number of barrels of oil each yielded. To simplify the keeping of records, little pictures were drawn of the whales. Half-whales, and those pictured with head down, represent the ones that escaped; captured whales are shown horizontally. On some ships, the pictures were not drawn, but stamped from wooden blocks. In the* Mary and Susan's *log, the catch of each boat is shown in a separate column. The whale at the top of the column at far right was unusually large, yielding 95 barrels of oil. Others yielded as little as six, but the average was around 40. Successful voyages were very profitable for owners and captains. The records of one ship that returned only two-thirds filled show that the owners made a huge profit—$850 for every $500 that they invested.*

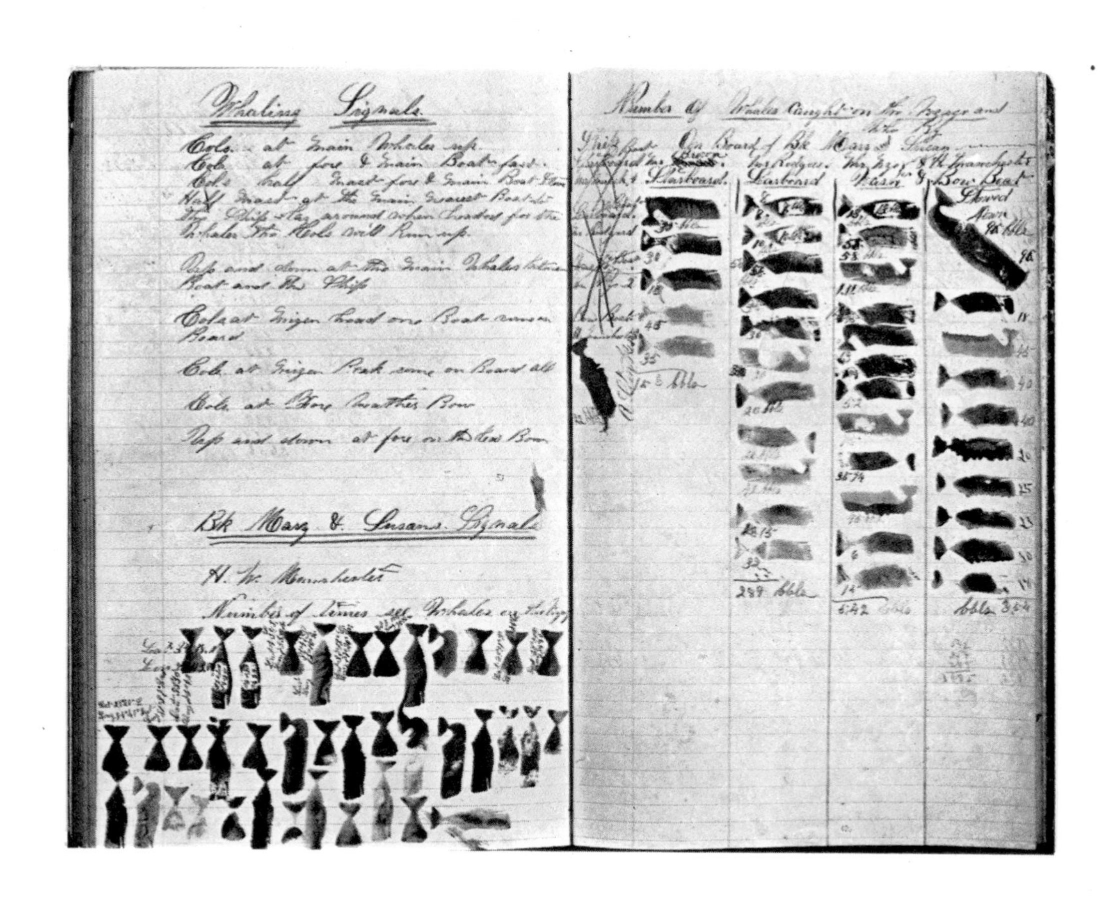

Whaling Signals.

Cols. at Main Whales up.
Cols at fore & Main Boat fast.
Cols half Mast fore & Main Boat Stove
Half Mast at the Main Mast Boat the
Ship stay around when headed for the
Whales the Cols will Run up.

Up and down at the Main Whales between
Boat and the Ship

Cols at Mizen head one Boat come on
Board

Cols at Mizen Peak come on Board all

Cols at Fore weather Bow

Up and down at fore on the lee Bow

Bk Mary & Susans Signals

H. W. Manchester

Numbers of times see Whales on the trip

Number of Whales Caught on the Voyage and the Bbl

On Board of Bk Mary & Susan

Starboard	Larboard	Waist	Bow Boat
15.6 bbls	289 bbls	542 bbls	bbls 354

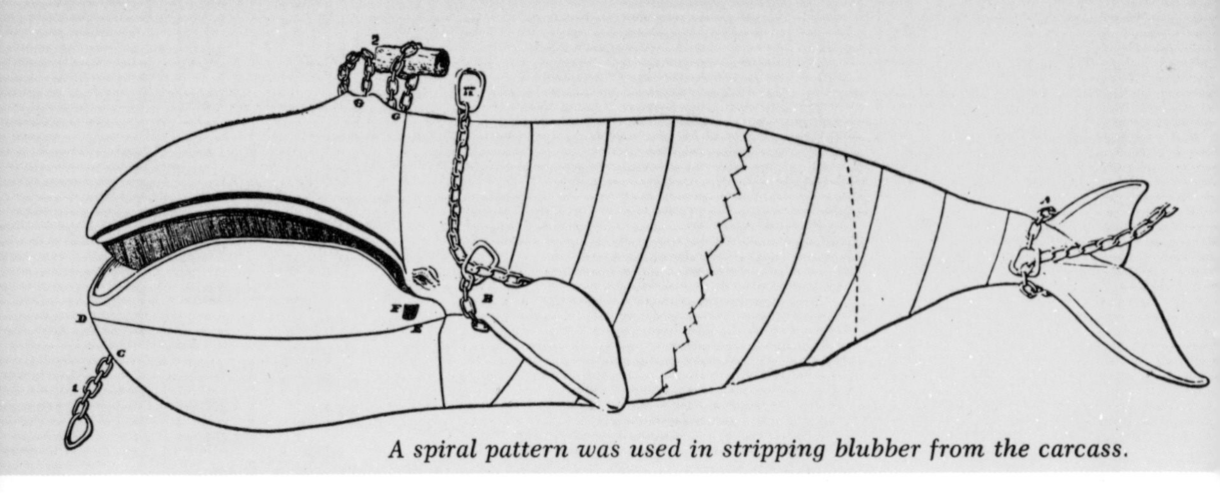

A spiral pattern was used in stripping blubber from the carcass.

To keep the line from running out too fast, he had taken a turn of it around a small post called a loggerhead. Pulled by the whale, the line passed around the loggerhead, hot and smoking from friction. An oarsman wet the line. The headsman took a few more turns around the loggerhead, the line grew tight, and the boat sped after the whale.

The headsman signaled to the harpooner, and the two changed places. This was a tricky thing to do in a bouncing, rocking boat, and it killed more than one man. The headsman went forward to kill the whale with a lance; the harpooner went aft to steer. There was no good reason for it. But it was a custom, handed down over the years. All whalemen learned it, few dared to break it, and the exchange was made on almost every chase.

What happened next was decided by the whale. If the whale "sounded," or dived deep, the men bobbed about on the water, keeping an eye on the line, until the whale breached. If the whale "ran" across the surface of the water, the men were off on a "Nantucket sleigh ride," sliding over the waves in a shower of spray.

Whatever the whale did, the men waited for it to grow tired. They pulled on the line, drawing the boat close enough so that the headsman could use his lance. He dug the sharp weapon deep, trying to "reach the life" of the whale—a tender spot, such as the lungs. He "churned" the lance up and down, until the whale spouted dark blood with every breath.

Mad with pain, the whale went into its "flurry." It swam furiously, around and around, in smaller and smaller circles. Then it beat the water with its tail, gave a tremendous shudder, and turned over on its back, fin out.

If there were more whales to catch, or more whaling ships in the neighborhood, the headsman stuck a "waif pole" into the whale. This was a pole with a flag of identification flying from it. No other ship would claim a whale that had been waifed. The dead whale floated in the water, an eighty-ton island of flesh and bone and blubber, topped with a little flag. This was done only with sperm whales. Bowhead whales, caught in the Arctic, had to be brought alongside the ship quickly or they would sink.

And so the chase ended—when everything went well. But often things did not go well. The crews of the whaleboats might row all day and never get within striking distance of a whale. The harpoon might not score a clean hit and the whale would escape. Lines could become tangled, boats could turn over in a storm. An "ugly" whale could attack its attackers, crushing a boat in its jaws or smashing it with a flip of its flukes. A Nantucket sleigh ride might take a boat too far for the ship ever to find it again.

And even if the chase had ended, the work had just begun. Because of the winds, it was not always possible for the ship to sail to the whale, and the two had to be brought together. The headsman made a hole in the whale's head with a cutting spade and attached a line. Then the tired, hungry men rowed again, towing the whale behind them. The gigantic corpse, the boats, the men bending over their oars, made a strange funeral procession under the evening sky.

And still the work was only just begun. The whale was made fast to the ship with heavy chains. Early the next day, the crew rigged a long, narrow platform over the whale for the "cutting-in." There was no time to lose. In southern waters, sharks gathered around the ship to feast on whale. With every bite they swallowed some of the profits of the voyage, and the men worked fast to keep from being robbed.

Cutting-in was a butcher's kind of job. The captain and the first mate stood on the cutting stage, as the long platform was called. They hacked at the whale with cutting spades, separating the head from the

The crew slice "horse pieces" of blubber into "Bible leaves" with mincing knife (at left).

In this whaling scene, painted by an unknown artist of the 1830's, cutting-in has begun at left, while oil smoke rises from the boiling try-pots of the ship at right.

body. The head, in turn, was divided into three parts. The twenty-ton "case" was full of the purest oil, which could be bailed out with a bucket. The "junk," the lower half of the forehead, would yield oil and spermaceti. Spermaceti was fatty matter, used for making fine candles and ointments. The jaw and teeth were saved for scrimshaw.

The second mate, too, was on the cutting stage. He cut the blubber into long strips. As the strips were hauled up on the deck, the whale turned around and around, while the blubber unwound like the peel of an orange. The strips were cut into "blanket pieces," weighing about a ton each. They were dropped through a hatch into the blubber room, where they were cut into blocks called "horse pieces."

When more than one whale had been caught, the work went on day and night, the men eating and sleeping in snatches. Oil, blood and grease were everywhere, on the deck, on the men, on their hands, on their clothes, on their bodies. The sea around the ship was stained. And in the stain a crowd of sharks splashed and snapped and fought for chunks of the whale.

Even dead, the whale was dangerous. Its juices made the deck and cutting stage slippery. A man could easily fall overboard to the sharks. Or he could be slashed by the sharp edge of a cutting spade, or crushed by a blanket piece swung through the air. The ship itself, rolling on the waves, swayed and creaked with the weight of the huge beast.

After most of the blubber had been stripped off, a mate poked in the body of the whale, searching

for treasure. He looked for ambergris, a substance used in the manufacture of perfume. Worth hundreds of dollars a pound, it was found only in sick whales. Few whalemen ever saw any, but they always searched and hoped.

Pulling aboard the last of the blanket pieces, the crew sang out "Five and forty more!"

Forty-five was the number of barrels of oil taken from the average whale. No matter what size the whale was, larger or smaller than average, the crew cried out, "Five and forty more! Five and forty mo-o-ore!"

The case and the junk were hauled up, and what was left of the whale was allowed to drift away.

"All hands aft to splice the mainbrace!" came the call from the captain.

As the blanket piece is hauled aboard, birds and sharks gather to feed on the whale.

This was one order the crew was happy to obey. They gathered around the captain, who poured a glass of grog for every man.

Cutting-in was over. It was time for the trying-out. The crew was divided into two watches, each taking six-hour turns of duty through the day and night.

A meal was dished out, then the first watch immediately went to work. Some of the men bailed out the oil from the case and tore the pulpy blubber from the sides. Other men went to the try-works and lighted a fire under the big try-pots. The fire was started with wood, but soon it would be fed with cracklings—scraps of blubber from which the oil had been boiled out.

"Bible leaves! Bible leaves!" shouted the men at the try-pots.

The rest of the watch were carrying horse pieces from the blubber room to the mincing block. Here thin slices were cut into the blocks of blubber, so that they looked like the leaves of a book. Bible leaves was the name the whalemen gave them, and Bible leaves were what they tossed into the try-pots.

For hours the whale cooked itself with the flames of its own cracklings. The ship was now a factory. But at night, blazing out of the darkness, it looked like some sea-going devil's floating kitchen, and the men like that devil's helpers. Black smoke rose higher than the masts. The sails reflected red fire. Over all, like an evil cloud, hung an immense stink of burning and boiling, of oil and blubber and blood and grease.

Dead, its bones lost, cut into

There was always danger that fire under the try-pots might spread. On many ships a wooden shelter built above the try-works stopped flying sparks and kept rain from falling into the boiling oil.

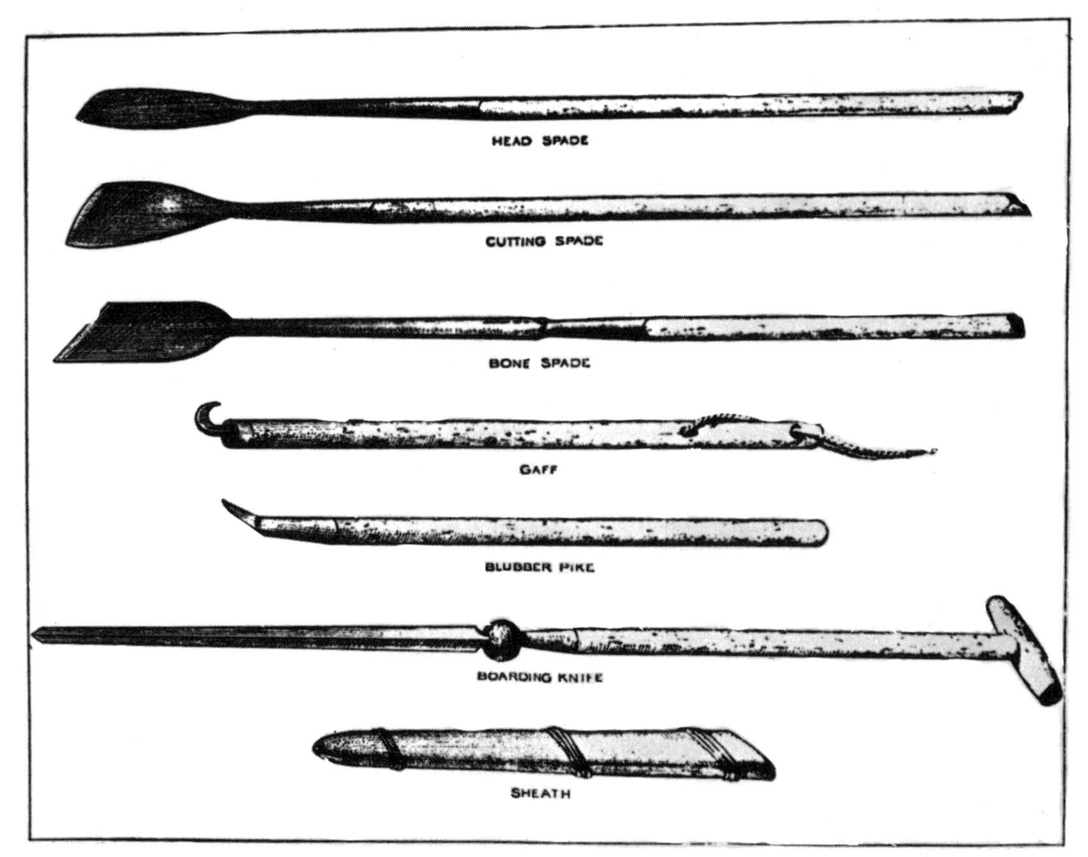

Spades and instruments used for cutting-in.

pieces and stewing in a pot, the whale was still dangerous. A high wave could splash scalding hot oil over the men around the try-works. Worse, the flame could spread and destroy the ship.

But at last every bit of blubber was tried out, the oil cooled, poured into barrels, and stowed in the hold. The crew swarmed over the ship in a big clean-up. They washed, they scrubbed, they scraped, they polished. They washed themselves and put on clean clothes. Except for the masts and sails, darkened by the greasy, sooty smoke of the try-works, the ship shone like something new.

Again lookouts were posted at the mastheads, watching for whales. Again would come the cry of "There she blows!" It might not happen for days, it might not happen for weeks —or it might happen within an hour. And so went life aboard a whaler, interrupted only by gams or storms or visits ashore—the watching and waiting, the chase, the cutting-in, the trying-out, the clean-up, the watching and waiting . . . until the captain gave the order: "All hands, to get the ship under way for home!"

Cutting-in on right whales captured in the North Pacific Ocean.

In Russell's panorama, the artist clearly shows the men perched on the cutting stage.

From the roofs of their houses, Nantucket wives watched for their husbands' ships.

WHALING CAPITALS

Thirty miles from the mainland, surrounded by the sea, lies the little island of Nantucket. The Indians told many stories of how it got there. Once the giant god Maushope lay down to rest on the sandy shore of Cape Cod. As he tossed and turned in his sleep, his moccasins filled with sand, and he angrily kicked them off. They fell into the ocean and became islands. One was later called Martha's Vineyard; the second, Nantucket.

In another story, a fierce eagle carried off Indian children from the mainland. After eating them, it dropped their bones in the water, and the pile of bones formed Nantucket. In still another story, the god Michabo knocked out the ashes of his pipe, and the heap of ashes was Nantucket.

But Nantucket first entered history in 1602, when Captain Bartholomew Gosnold discovered Cape Cod. Exploring the waters south of the Cape, he found a number of islands, including Nantucket and Martha's

Vineyard. He claimed them all for England.

By 1641 the islands were owned by two English lords, who sold them to Thomas Mayhew. A rich merchant from the Massachusetts Bay Colony, Mayhew was a Puritan and a deeply religious man. He longed to bring Christianity to the Indians, and he started with the friendly Gay Head tribe on Martha's Vineyard. Mayhew treated them well, and soon the Vineyard had a small settlement of whites.

Back in the Massachusetts colony, the Puritans were less kind to people of other beliefs than Mayhew was to the Indians. They had come to America for freedom of religion, but they saw no need of it for anyone else. Their laws were hard on Baptists, Anabaptists, Presbyterians, and especially on Quakers, whom they sometimes hanged.

Tristram Coffin and Thomas Macy decided to leave the colony and find a new home. Seven other men joined them in a company to buy Nantucket, where they could raise sheep for wool. Mayhew's price was thirty pounds and "also two Beaver Hatts one for myself and one for my wife."

Before Thomas Macy left Massachusetts, he broke one of the Puritans' laws. On a rainy morning four Quakers came to his door, asking the way to a neighboring town. Macy was a Baptist, but he would keep no one, not even a Quaker, standing in the rain. He invited the strangers into his house to wait until the storm was over. This was against the law. Anyone having Quakers in his house could be fined forty shillings for every hour they stayed. Macy told the Court that the four Quakers were in his house about three-quarters of an hour, and he was fined thirty shillings.

More sure than ever that he was doing the right thing, Macy set out

As Quakers forbade pictures, this earliest view of Nantucket was not made until 1810.

In 1848 New Bedford was the world's greatest whaling port, with a fine harbor deep enough for the largest whaling vessels. This view shows the city as seen from Fairhaven, its sister port on the Acushnet River's opposite bank.

for Nantucket in the fall of 1659. He made the journey in a small sloop. With him went his wife and five children, as well as Edward Starbuck, and a boy named Isaac Coleman. A high wind came up, the sloop rocked in the waves, and Mrs. Macy wanted to turn back.

"Woman," Thomas Macy said, "go below and seek thy God. I fear not the witches on earth or the devils in hell!"

There were neither witches nor devils waiting on Nantucket's sandy shore. There were only Indians, and they were friendly. They helped Macy's small party get through the winter, and in spring eight or ten more families came to the island. Year by year, the settlement grew. The settlers raised sheep, they farmed a little, they fished—and they whaled.

In 1690 several Nantucketers were standing on a hill, looking at the whales spouting and playing in the water. One man pointed to the sea.

"There," he said, "is a green pasture where our children's grandchildren will go for bread."

But already there were masts along the shore, from which lookouts watched for whales. Already there were crews that went out in small boats, captured whales, towed them in, and boiled their blubber for oil. Fifteen years later even more Nantucketers were going to the green pasture of the sea for their bread. And by that time something else had come to Nantucket. It was Quakerism, and, along with whaling, it would shape the lives of the people for many years to come.

Although most of the islanders were Baptists and Presbyterians, they listened willingly to the preaching of any minister who

visited them. They even listened to the missionaries sent by the Quakers, and among the listeners was Mary Starbuck. Mary and her husband, Nathaniel, owned the biggest and finest house on Nantucket. Part of the house was a store, where the couple sold "powder, shot, flints, sope, shuse, molasses, board and nails," cloth, buttons, thread, wine, rum, beer, cider, and anything else that could be brought from the mainland. Gatherings to talk over the town's business were held in the house so often that the Nantucketers usually called it "Parliament House."

Everyone thought well of the Starbucks and took notice of what they said. Because of her good sense, Mary was known as "the Great Mary" or "the Great Woman." And when she became a Quaker, many of her neighbors followed her example. Some Nantucketers still remained Baptists or Presbyterians or "Nothingarians" who belonged to no church. But at least half the island belonged to the Society of Friends, as the Quakers called themselves.

Like Quakers everywhere, those on Nantucket believed in honesty, thrift, and hard work. They were against war and fighting. They would have no unnecessary decoration on their houses, and they dressed in the plainest of clothes. The men wore dark, homespun suits and square-toed shoes. The women wore simple dresses, shawls and bonnets. They used the words "thee" and "thou" instead of "you," and they allowed no music, dancing or card-playing in their homes.

And so it happened that on Nantucket, whalemen became Quakers, and Quakers became whalemen. Believing in peace, they yet made war on whales, and their battlefields were the waters of the world. Hating gambling, they yet gambled their lives on the toss of a harpoon, and their fortunes on ships that might never return. Loving a quiet life, they yet knew storm and shipwreck, mutiny and piracy, and bloody deeds of savages and cannibals. Mistrusting amusements and pleasures, they yet heard strange music and watched wild dancing, in distant lands smelling of spice.

But Quakerism taught them thrift, and there was money in whaling. Quakerism taught them to work hard, and there was hard work in whaling. Quakerism taught them courage and patience, and there was need of courage and patience in whaling.

At first, when voyages were short, the blubber was cut up, packed into barrels, and brought back to Nantucket to be tried out. The stink of blubber and boiling oil mingled with the fog that often covered the island, or rose into the salt air the winds brought from the sea. Around 1730, as the voyages became longer, try-works were built on the ships themselves. The stink of boiling oil gave way to the sweetish smell of oil stored in casks and carried ashore.

Nantucket went on growing. In 1775 it had 4500 people and owned 150 vessels. Life was pleasant until the American Revolution put a halt to whaling. Between the Revolution and the War of 1812, Nantucket grew again. And, after the War of 1812, began the greatest days of Nantucket whaling. From this small island, no longer than fifteen miles, no wider than five, ships went sailing to all the waters of the globe. By 1840, at least one whaler entered or left the harbor every week, and every day there were ships tied up at the wharves, unloading or preparing for a voyage. Always the tall masts of whalers punctuated the sky over the waterfront. And between the shadows of the masts and the gently rocking hulls darted smaller vessels and boats, carrying supplies.

On the land, too, men who never went to sea made their living from

Whales spout on the horizon in this imaginative picture (above) of Marblehead, a New England seaport. William A. Wall's famous picture (below), "New Bedford Fifty Years Ago," was painted in 1857. The large building is on the corner of what are now Union and Water Streets. Off to the left rises Johnnycake Hill, where today stand the Seamen's Bethel and the Whaling Museum of the Old Dartmouth Historical Society. The large man with the white vest is William Rotch, Jr., the town's leading merchant.

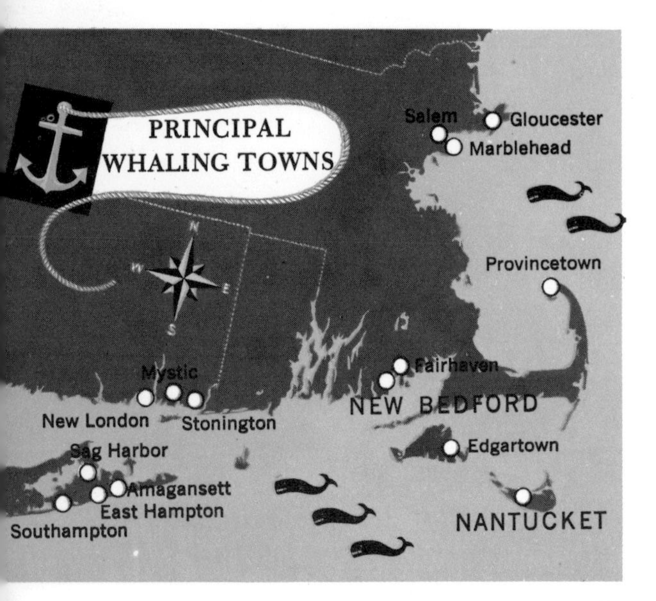

Nantucket and New Bedford were the world's most important whaling towns.

the whale. They drove wagons and carts over the cobblestones, hauling oil casks to warehouses. They worked in sail lofts, making and repairing sails; in ropewalks, weaving lines of rope; in blacksmith shops, forging harpoons and lances; in coopers' shops, in carpenters' shops, in candle factories; in hardware and grocery shops that sold supplies to whalers.

On upper Main Street were the big houses of whaling merchants and captains, with "walks" on the roofs (later known as "widow's walks") where wives could watch for incoming ships. And there were many wives left to watch, for most voyages lasted three or four years. Nantucketers liked to tell the story of a captain who was sailing on a short voyage. When he was on his ship, he remembered that he had not said good-bye to his wife.

"Well, no matter," he said, "I am only to be gone two years."

Some of the islanders still raised sheep, but most of Nantucket lived by the whale and for the whale. Often a Nantucket girl would refuse to marry a man until he had gone on a whaling voyage.

To make the voyages more profitable, larger ships were built. They carried more oil and made more money, but they meant the end of Nantucket whaling. For across the island's harbor was a sand bar, and the water here was too shallow for larger ships to cross.

The Nantucketers built a "camel" —a sort of barge or floating drydock, pulled by a small steamboat—with which to float ships over the bar. In 1842, a crowd welcomed the first ship to come into the harbor on the camel, and the next few years were the greatest Nantucket had ever known.

But already sperm whales were becoming hard to find. Whalemen began sailing to the Arctic waters, to hunt the right and the humpback whale. Ships needed larger crews, and were built still larger—too large to enter Nantucket's harbor. Nantucket had other misfortunes, too. In 1846 fire destroyed most of the business district, and in 1849 many of the young men left for California to find gold. Many

A whaling vessel drying out its sails at a dock in New Bedford, around 1880.

families moved away, and fewer and fewer ships came into the harbor. As whaling died, so did Quakerism. In 1869 the last Nantucket whaler set sail, never to return. A great quiet seemed to fall over the town, over the rotting wharves and deserted warehouses, over the little gray houses and the fine mansions of the merchants. By 1875 there were only 3,000 people left of the 10,000 who had once lived on the island. That quiet was not broken until the 1880's, when Nantucket became a summer resort. Visitors strolled down the tree-lined streets, and the town began a different life.

Whaling vessels had gone out from Provincetown, on Cape Cod; from Sag Harbor, on Long Island; from Edgartown, on Martha's Vineyard; from New London and Mystic and Stonington, in Connecticut. But

On New Bedford's waterfront, whale-oil gaugers tested the quality and quantity of oil.

it was New Bedford, in Massachusetts, that replaced Nantucket as the whaling capital of the world.

Like Nantucket, New Bedford was discovered by Captain Bartholomew Gosnold in 1602. On the west bank of the Acushnet River, where the town would be built, he saw "stately groves, flowering meadows, and running brooks." He was met by Indians "who with all courteous kindness entertained him, giving him skins of wild beasts, tobacco, turtles, hemp, artificial strings colored [wampum] and such like things as they had about them."

Like Nantucket, New Bedford was settled by people who wanted religious freedom. Many of them were Quakers. Again like Nantucket, New

Bedford knew hardship during the Revolution, when it was set on fire by British raiders, and during the War of 1812. Unlike Nantucket, it had a harbor deep enough for the largest ships.

New Bedford whaling began in the 1750's. In 1765, Joseph Rotch, who had already become rich as a whaling merchant in Nantucket, moved to New Bedford. There he carried on the business of whaling, as did Joseph Russel, one of the founders of the village. They built ships, sent them out on whaling voyages, and were dealers in the products of whaling. Together they gave New Bedford its start as a whaling port.

The greatest days came in the years from 1825 to 1860. Tall-masted ships crowded the harbor, and the wharves were lined with casks of oil giving off a heavy, sweet smell. Merchants in high silk hats and long-tailed coats picked their way across the oil-soaked ground. They checked their cargoes and gave orders to workmen, who covered the casks with seaweed to protect them from the weather.

On the streets sloping down to the waterfront were substantial buildings where the merchants had their counting rooms, or offices. Next to them were the banks, the insurance companies, the law offices, and warehouses, oil refineries, and shops of dealers in oil, bone and spermaceti. All were connected with whaling. No wonder that Ralph Waldo Emerson, who preached for a time in New Bedford, said that "they have all the equipment for a whaler ready, and they hug an oil cask like a brother."

This section of Russell's panorama depicts the steamer Massachusetts *towing the whaler* Niger *past Clark's Lighthouse into home port in New Bedford harbor.*

FISH
MARKET

After the Civil War, New Bedford harbor was crowded with idle whaling vessels. This photograph was taken in 1869.

Here, too, as in Nantucket, were the shops of coopers, sailmakers, riggers, ropemakers, blacksmiths, carpenters, chandlers. The shops were always busy. One blacksmith, James Durfee, made 58,517 harpoons during his lifetime. Another, a Negro named Lewis Temple, invented a harpoon called the Temple Toggle Iron that was used by every whaler. Bakeries specializing in dry, hard, ship's bread turned out thousands of loaves from their brick ovens.

Atop Johnnycake Hill stood the Seaman's Bethel, a church for whalemen. Nearby, usually on the second floor of shop buildings, were the sailors' boarding houses, smelling of clam and fish chowder. Scattered about were taverns and grog shops. In front of them, on the cobbled streets, ambled whalemen of two dozen different nations, including former cannibals from the South Seas.

A little distance from the waterfront, out of the smell of whale oil, were the mansions of the rich merchants. The widow's walks on the roofs overlooked streets with green trees and lawns and hedges and fragrant gardens. Sailors said that, after a voyage, walking these shaded streets was like a trip into the country. And yet in the houses,

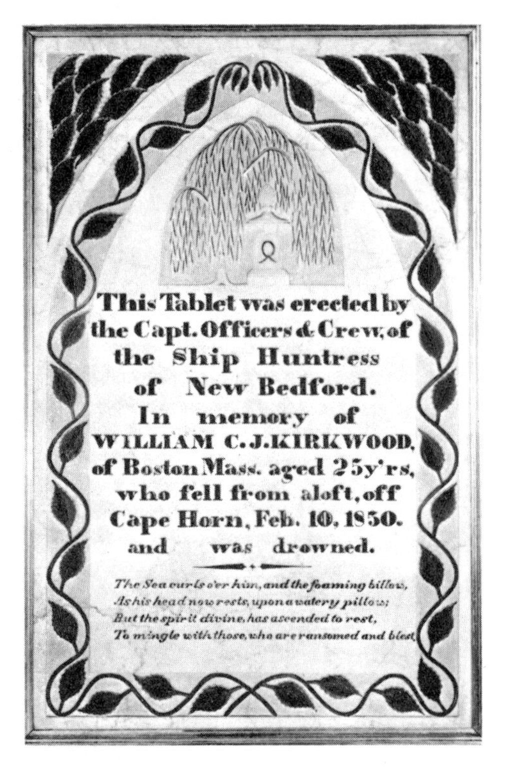

A memorial for a drowned sailor, from the Seamen's Bethel, the old whalemen's church still standing in New Bedford.

Joseph Starbuck, prominent whaling merchant of Nantucket, built three fine houses (opposite) for his sons.

perhaps on the polished top of a table next to a horsehair sofa, could be found *The Whalemen's Shipping List and Merchant's Transcript*, a weekly paper. It was said that the attics held huge barrels of oil to be burned for special celebrations, and that the merchants often gave their daughters a whale for a wedding present.

Near the wharves, on Water and Union streets, were the outfitters' shops. They sold clothes, hats and shoes for whalemen. Whenever a ship that had had "greasy luck" came in, the men on board would have one or two hundred dollars in their pockets—and the outfitters wanted their share. Each of them had runners, called "landsharks" by the whalemen, who met the incoming ships.

The sharks spent much of the day in the lookout towers of the shops. They watched the lighthouse in the harbor, which hung out a yardarm as soon as a ship was sighted.

"The arm is out!" the sharks would cry. The news spread through town—"The arm is out!"—and crowds rushed to the waterfront, to greet their friends and relatives on the whaler, or to get word from its crew of other ships. But the sharks reached the ship first, racing to it on a "shark boat." Besides selling outfits to the sailors, they hoped to persuade them to make a voyage on another ship.

For whaling needed men, and New Bedford was out to get them. In towns throughout the East, notices were posted:

LANDSMEN WANTED!!

One thousand stout young men, Americans, wanted for the fleet of whaleships, now fitting out for the North and South Pacific Fisheries.

Extra chances given to Coopers, Carpenters, and Blacksmiths.

None but industrious young men, with good recommendations, taken. Such will have superior chances for advancement.

Outfits, to the amount of seventy-five dollars furnished to each individual, before proceeding to sea.

Persons desirous to avail themselves of the present splendid opportunity of seeing the world, and at the same time acquiring a profitable business, will do well to make early application to the undersigned.

And the greenhorns came to New Bedford—farm boys and town boys and city boys, eager for adventure. Sharks and agents outfitted them, paid their boardinghouse bills, and

Homes of Starbuck's three sons are called East Brick, Middle Brick and West Brick.

A steamer tows a whaler on the "camel," a barge or floating drydock, used in Nantucket from 1842 to 1849, to get large vessels over the sandbar at the harbor's mouth.

watched them sharply. Not until the greenies were aboard ship, and the ship sailing, did the sharks get their money and their profit from the shipowners. The owners could not lose, for the money would come out of the greenhorn's lay.

Sharks and boardinghouse keepers often did the same sort of thing with experienced whalemen. Sometimes, to make sure the whaleman would turn up at the ship, he would be thrown into jail for debt and let out only when his ship sailed. Some whalemen said that the jail was more comfortable than the boardinghouses.

New Bedford's greatest whaling year was 1857. Ten thousand men were making their living in the whaling industry. The fleet of 329 vessels brought in oil and bone worth $6,178,728. Then, slowly, over the years, the fleet grew smaller. In 1861, during the Civil War, the forty vessels of the "Stone Fleet" were destroyed. The government ordered the ships loaded with stones and sunk in Southern harbors in an attempt to block off Confederate shipping. A large number of other whalers were sunk by the guns of the Confederate cruisers, the *Alabama* and the *Shenandoah*. In 1871 thirty-three ships were crushed in the ice of the Arctic; in 1876, twelve more.

Besides, whales were becoming harder to find. Voyages had to be still longer, and that meant even bigger crews. But the real beginning of the end for whaling came in 1859. That year, petroleum—"rock oil," as people called it—was discovered in Pennsylvania. During the late 1800's, the use of petroleum and natural gas for lighting quickly spread. The world no longer needed

Casks of whale oil were covered with seaweed to protect them from the weather.

whale oil for its lamps. And celluloid replaced whalebone for use as stays in women's corsets.

In New Bedford, the coopers' shops, the riggers' shops, the carpenters' shops closed, one by one. Old ships, their masts bare as the bones of skeletons, were left to rot at the wharves.

Business men who looked ahead put their money into factories for making cloth. Hundreds of Portuguese whalemen settled in New Bedford and went to work in the mills or in the fishing boats. A faint smell of whale oil, heavy and sweet, lingered for a while in the earth of the waterfront, and then it, too, was gone.

In August of 1925 the schooner *John R. Manta*, the last of the whalers to sail from New Bedford, completed its last voyage. The days of whaling under sail were over.

When whaling ended, New Bedford's waterfront was silent and deserted.

The whaler Kutusoff, *on which Benjamin Russell sailed around the world.*

ADVENTURE ON THE FAR WATERS

From lane to lane, from street to street, from house to house, the news spread over Nantucket:

"Did thee hear, neighbor? A ship has been sighted. Some think she may be a Cape Horner."

Although it was March—March of 1793—and the chill of winter still clung to the island, men, women and children rushed outside. They stood on the highest hilltops, they stood on the roofs of

Yankees saw natives of many lands, such as these Africans whaling off Zanzibar.

their houses, watching for the ship.

At last Thaddeus Joy, who had a good eye for such things, spoke up. By the cut of her sails, he judged the vessel to be the *Beaver*. Aye, and her master was Paul Worth.

Later that day, the seventeen men of her crew came ashore. They had sailed around Cape Horn, where the ocean exploded with storms and spray froze into ice on the sails. And only a month before, the *Rebecca* had returned to New Bedford after rounding the Horn. The *Beaver* and the *Rebecca* were the first whalers to enter the Pacific from American ports.

◄ *The voyages of whalers often took them past the island of Fogo, in the Cape Verde Islands off the west coast of Africa, which was the site of an active volcano.*

Not that there was anything new about whalemen traveling to places dangerous or unknown. The hunt for whales took them to the far waters of the earth, and they were forced to be discoverers, explorers and pathfinders. At first they had pushed out into the Atlantic, north to the Davis Straits, south to the Brazil Banks and the Indian Ocean. Then, rounding the Horn, they went on to the Pacific. They discovered dozens of small islands and gave them Yankee names. They were among the first white men to see the fearful stone faces of Easter Island, the dancing girls of Hawaii, the glaring snowfields of the Antarctic. Farther north they sailed, to the waters of Japan, to the whaling grounds

Two views of the Azores from Russell's panorama. Whalers usually stopped here or at the Cape Verde Islands to take on fresh fruit, vegetables, and water. Both groups of islands were owned by Portugal. Captains often filled out their crews with Portuguese islanders, many of whom later settled permanently in New Bedford.

called Kodiak and Kamchatka, and into the Arctic Ocean itself. From the beginning, they studied the ocean currents, and the secrets of the sea became the secrets of their trade—all in the hunt for whales.

Benjamin Franklin, himself the grandson of a Nantucketeer, knew this. When he wanted to learn about the Gulf Stream, he went to his whaleman cousin, Captain Timothy Folger. The captain drew him a sketch of the Stream, which had never before been mapped. Franklin published it in 1786, explaining that the Nantucket whalemen were "extremely well acquainted with the Gulf Stream . . .

A native of the Sandwich Islands—the former name of the Hawaiian Islands.

by their constant practice of whaling on the edges of it, from their island quite down to the Bahamas."

Whatever else they did, whalemen never forgot that they were hunters. During the years of 1785 to 1810, sealskins were bringing a good price in China, and many whalemen turned to hunting seals and sea-elephants. At islands like those in the Falklands and South Georgia, they went ashore and found huge herds of the animals. The crews clubbed them to death,

Horseracing on Zanzibar, sketched by J. Ross Browne on a whaling cruise in 1845.

Whalemen saw many strange sights, such as this dance on Tahiti in the Society Islands.

skinned them, and scraped the skins. They boiled the blubber of sea-elephants into oil, often in try-pots set up on the beach.

Whaling was a business, an industry. Captured whales furnished blubber, which was made into oil, which was sold for cash. Whaling had its risks, but it could pay, and pay well. Some captains retired before the age of forty. Some ships, costing ten thousand dollars, returned from their voyage with a cargo worth twenty thousand. In their counting rooms at Nantucket and New Bedford, the whaling merchants reckoned the success of a voyage in dollars and cents. Adventure was an accident. Too often, it interfered with whaling and cut down on profits. And yet, hunting on the far waters, whalemen could not help but meet with adventure.

There was Captain Mayhew Folger, for instance, who found himself part of one of the strangest tales in the history of the sea. Captain Folger was a Nantucketer, and in 1807 he took the *Topaz*, a Boston ship, out on a sealing voyage. Hoping to come across islands where no sealing had ever been done, he cruised the South Atlantic. He failed to find any seals, and in

1808 he sailed to the South Pacific. Here, too, his luck was bad, and in February he made for Pitcairn Island to get fresh water. Pitcairn Island had been discovered in 1767 and had not been visited since.

Anchoring the *Topaz* a little distance from the island, Captain Folger set out with two whaleboats to explore the land. He was surprised to see smoke rising from the shore. According to his information, Pitcairn had never been inhabited. Even more surprising, he saw a crude canoe coming toward him, paddled by three men. They were dressed like natives, and looked like natives, but there was something different about them.

And then one of them spoke, and he spoke in English. "What ship is that?" he said slowly. "Where do you come from?"

"It is the ship *Topaz*, of the United States of America. I am Mayhew Folger, her master, an American."

"You are an American? You come from America? Where is America? Is it in Ireland?"

Captain Folger peered at the men. He asked, "Who are you?"

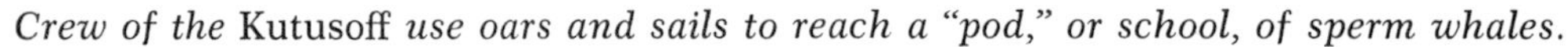

Crew of the Kutusoff *use oars and sails to reach a "pod," or school, of sperm whales.*

"We are Englishmen."

"Where were you born?"

One of the men in the canoe motioned toward the land. "On that island, which you see."

"How, then, are you Englishmen, if you were born on that island, which the English do not own and never possessed?"

"We are Englishmen because our father was an Englishman."

"Who is your father?"

"Aleck," said the men.

Captain Folger was growing more and more puzzled. "Who is Aleck?" he said.

"Don't you know Aleck? Well, then, do you know Captain Bligh of the *Bounty?*"

And suddenly Captain Folger knew who these men were. What seaman had not heard of the *Bounty*, and talked about it, and thought about it, and wondered about it? The *Bounty* was an English naval ship commanded by Captain William Bligh. The crew had mutinied against his harsh treatment. Bligh and eighteen of his men were set adrift in a small boat; they reached Timor after traveling about 4000 miles. Six of the muti-

Russell's panorama here exaggerates the rugged mountains of the Marquesas Islands.

Yankee whalemen cruised the waters of the South Pacific almost fifty years before they had been explored and charted. This picture of Sydney, Australia, was not made until 1842, when Charles Wilkes, an American naval officer, led an official expedition which charted little-known regions of the world.

neers were captured in Tahiti. They were put on trial in England and three were hanged. But what had happened to the other mutineers? For twenty years the world had wondered, and now Captain Folger was about to find out.

On shore, he met Aleck—Alexander Smith—and heard his story. Folger returned to his ship and wrote in the log that Smith and eight other mutineers had first gone to Tahiti, where they all took wives and six men as servants. Then they settled on Pitcairn Island, breaking up the *Bounty*. Soon after that, "one of their party ran mad and drowned himself another died with a fever, and after they had remained about 4 years on the Island their Men Servants rose upon & killed Six of them, Leaving only Smith & he desperately wounded with a pistol Ball in the neck, however he & the widows of the deceased men arose and put all the Servants to death which left him the only Surviving man on the Island with 8 or 9 women and Several Small Children." And three children had grown into the men Folger had seen in the canoe.

Nukualofa was in the Tonga Islands, near Samoa, where whalers often visited.

Quaker whalemen visited exotic places of worship such as this Singapore temple.

Folger stayed at Pitcairn for two days, then set sail for South America—but his adventures were not over. At Juan Fernández Island, the *Topaz* was fired upon by the cannons of the Spanish governor. Folger and all his crew were made prisoners, while the ship was robbed. Folger was taken to Valparaíso, and had to travel by land to Santiago before he could arrange to get his ship back. Not until the end of 1808 did he bring the *Topaz* into her home port.

She was not the only ship that had trouble with the Spanish who ruled most of South America. In 1820, the whaler *Hero* put in at the bay of Santa Maria in Chile. Her captain, James Russell, was invited to visit General Benevedes, the Spanish commandant. After a good dinner, General Benevedes accused the captain of spying for the Chileans who wanted to overthrow Spanish rule, and had him jailed.

NAVIGATORS

These natives of New Holland—one of the early names used for Australia—were sketched on a whaling voyage in 1842.

These boatmen of the South Pacific are pictured here off one of the Fiji Islands.

Meanwhile, soldiers swarmed over the *Hero*. They took off three of the crew, tied up the rest in the forecastle, and robbed the ship. Then they cut the anchor cable and let the ship drift toward the rocky shore.

Obed Starbuck, the eighteen-year-old mate, managed to free himself.

"Come on, boys!" he said. "Let's get her out to sea!"

The crew got the ship under control just in time to keep her from crashing on the rocks. Starbuck brought the *Hero* to Valparaíso, and then to Nantucket. He was made captain on the ship's next voyage.

Captain Russell and the cabin boy were killed by Benevedes, who was no better than a pirate. He attacked other ships, and later the people of Chile rose up against him and cut off his head.

The year that the whaler *Hero* met adventure in Chile, another vessel of the same name met adventure in a different part of the world. This *Hero* was a small sloop, and her captain was twenty-one-year-old Nathaniel Brown Palmer. On a sealing voyage with a fleet from Stonington, Connecticut, he was searching the cold waters below South America. On November eighteenth he brought the ship into "a strait . . . filled with Ice" and, as the fog lifted, he saw the frozen cliffs of a new continent—Antarctica.

Nat Palmer may not have known that he had found a continent. But several months later, Captain John Davis of New Haven, Connecticut, and Captain Christopher Burdick of Nantucket were also cruising these waters. Captain Burdick, of the schooner *Huntress*, wrote in his log: "Land from South to ESE which I suppose to be a Continent."

In the hot places of the world as well as the cold, whalemen met adventure. In 1851 the *Charles W. Morgan* of New Bedford was in the South Pacific. A calm had fallen over the sea, and the rising sun filled the sky with flame. Heat seemed to gather about the ship, sucking up the water the crew had poured on deck in the morning clean-up. Into the deadly silence a lookout called, "Land-ho!"

The current was carrying them toward Sydenham Island. The natives were savages who had captured more than one ship, killing the crews or holding them to be ransomed by the next whaler for a few boxes of tobacco. Every man aboard knew that if a wind did not rise, there would be no escape. And a wind did not rise.

Soldiers from the French fort on Tahiti welcomed the Kutusoff's *crew.*

"Here they come!" cried the lookout on the mainmast.

Paddling canoes, the natives made for the ship. They carried swords and spears made of shark's teeth fastened to cocoanut wood.

Captain Sampson had the ship's firearms—a few muskets and revolvers, and a shotgun—brought on deck. He ordered the crew to stand along the rail with lances and cutting spades.

"Keep them off the ship," he said. "But do not kill any if you can avoid it."

For an hour or more the canoes kept coming, until at least five hundred natives surrounded the ship. They yelled, they jabbered, they shouted insults, they shook their fists and raised their weapons. Once they tried to rush the ship, but they were driven off by the sharp cutting spades.

Few whalers cruised the Pacific without putting in at Honolulu, shown here in 1854.

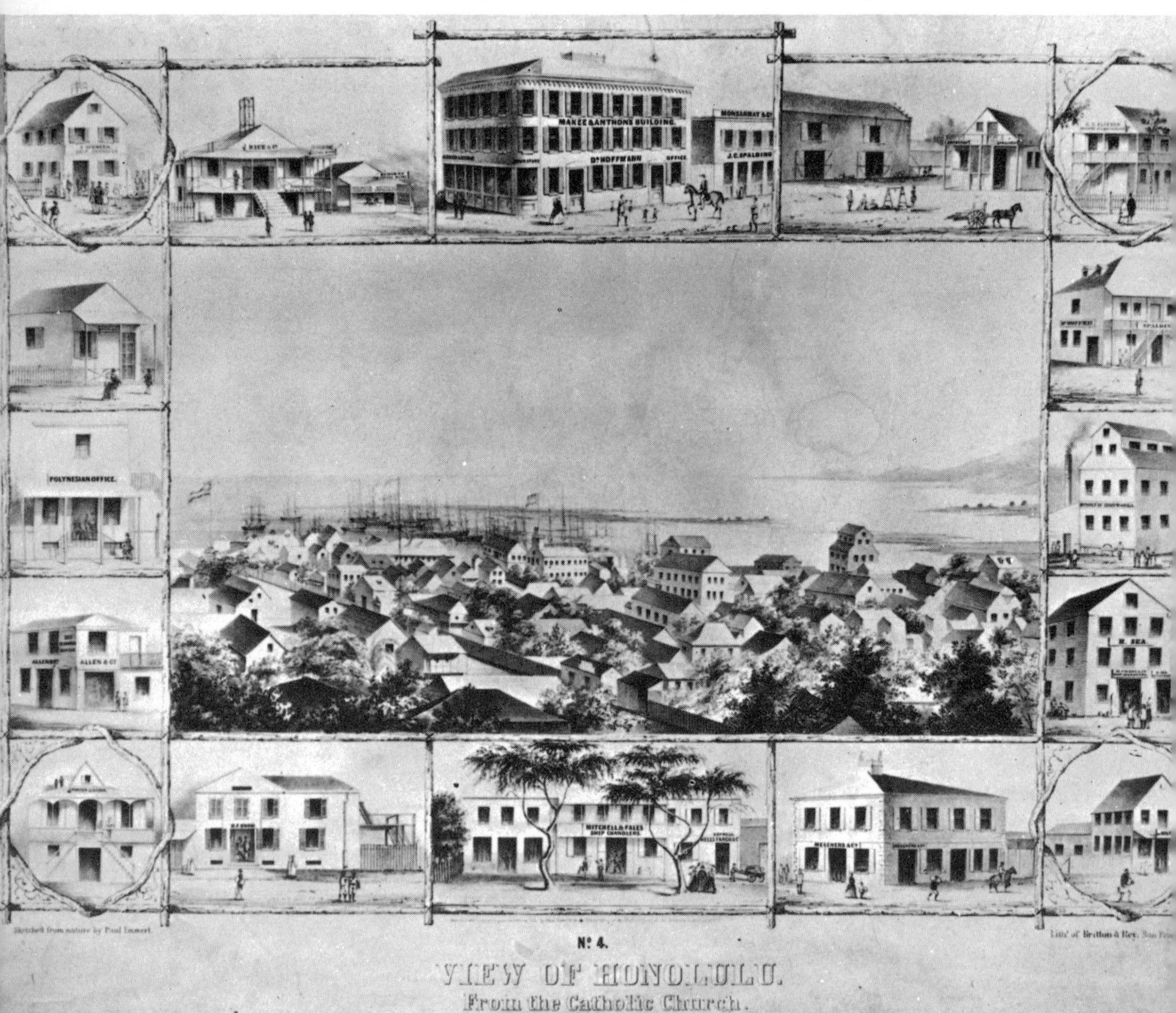

The harbor at Lahaina, in the Hawaiians, was often crowded with whaling vessels. Hawaii's native rulers, in power until 1893, encouraged trade with Americans.

The captain paced the quarter deck, a musket in his hand. He was in full sight of the crowd, and many of the insults were for him. A native would stand up in a canoe, turn his back on the captain, and make a low bow. Muttering angrily to himself, the captain exchanged his musket for a shotgun.

One canoe shoved out from the rest. A dignified native, wearing a large white shell on a string around his neck, stood up. Slowly he turned his back on the captain. With his hands on his hips, he bowed low. Raising his gun, the captain fired, sending a charge of buckshot into the native's backside. Still dignified, the native dived into the water and swam off.

For a while there was silence. Then, with a great shout, the natives rushed the ship again—and again they were driven off. This time some of them were cut on the hands, arms, shoulders and head, and they left streaks of blood on the side of the ship.

The ship was drifting closer and closer to the island. The whalemen could see the white beach, the crowds of men, women and children moving among the cocoanut trees and the grass houses.

The First Mate called out from the bows, "Here is a patch of coral

An initiation ceremony (above) for whalemen crossing the equator for the first time. Under the direction of a sailor holding a trident and dressed as Neptune, king of the sea, the blindfolded victims were doused with water, lathered with an unpleasant soapy mixture, shaved with a huge razor, and tricked into believing they had been tossed overboard. The illustration (below) from Harper's Weekly *of May, 1874, shows seamen clubbing seals to death. Many whalers hunted seals as well as whales.*

Whaling and sealing in the Davis Straits, between Greenland and Baffin Island

right across our bows just under water! The ship can never get over it!"

"How far are we from it?" the Captain asked.

"Only about three ship's lengths."

"How much on each bow?"

"On the starboard bow I can see no end," the Mate said. "On the port bow about four points is the outer end."

The men of the crew looked at each other. In a few minutes the ship would be stranded on the reef. The natives in the canoes stood up, shrieking. They threw their paddles into the air, caught them, and shook them like war clubs. On shore, too, the natives shrieked and howled, jumped and danced about.

And then, unbelievably, the ship began to turn and drift away from the island. Carried by the current, she cleared the reef. In a half hour she was in deep water, and the natives were quietly paddling their canoes back to shore. The whalemen shouted and gestured at them, fired the guns and pistols, and gave three cheers. The next morning a fresh breeze swelled the sails. Acting like schoolboys on a holiday, the crew laughed and grinned and skylarked. The danger was over and they could go back to the business of whaling.

As sperm whales became hard to find, the whalers sailed farther and farther north on the Pacific. In 1848 Captain James Royce of Sag Harbor brought his bark *Superior* up the Bering Sea, in the Arctic, and found bowhead whales. New Bedford ships followed soon after, and among them was the *Citizen.* In the Arctic Ocean, a storm sent her crashing upon the rocks and the surf began to rip her to pieces. The crew reached shore, built a fire, and spent the night in casks and a tent made of bits of sails. It was August, and they knew there would be no ship to rescue them until the Arctic winter was over.

Setting off across the land, they found a small Eskimo village. All winter they lived with the Eskimos in their little huts made of animal skins. The Eskimos enjoyed hearing the whalemen sing. While the wind howled in the darkness, and the Northern Lights flared above the frozen rim of the world, the crew sang for them—mostly hymns like *Beulah Land* and *Blessed Be the Tie That Binds.*

When they began to run out of food, they set off again across the land. After traveling 250 miles on foot, they were rescued by a whaler in the spring, and by April of 1865 they finally reached home.

Unlike the sperm whale, the bowhead of the Arctic was no fighter.

Hunting for right whales in the Bering Strait, between Siberia and Alaska, in 1871. Just four years earlier, the United States had purchased Alaska from Russia.

A whaler among icebergs—a constant danger in the foggy waters of the Arctic. No whalers were ever painted white; the hull of this vessel is coated with frozen spray

In the northern regions, the whaleman's enemy was not the whale, but the Arctic itself. He had to fight the cold, the wind and the ice—and he had to outwit the seasons. He had to wait until the ice melted in mid-summer to sail up the Bering Straits into the Arctic Ocean. And he had to sail out in September or early October, before the sea froze over again.

In 1871, an unexpected southwest wind brought snow and cold at the end of August. Before a week had passed, the ice began closing in. Thirty-three ships, twenty-two of them from New Bedford, were trapped, locked in the crushing grip of the ice. *(Continued on page 92)*

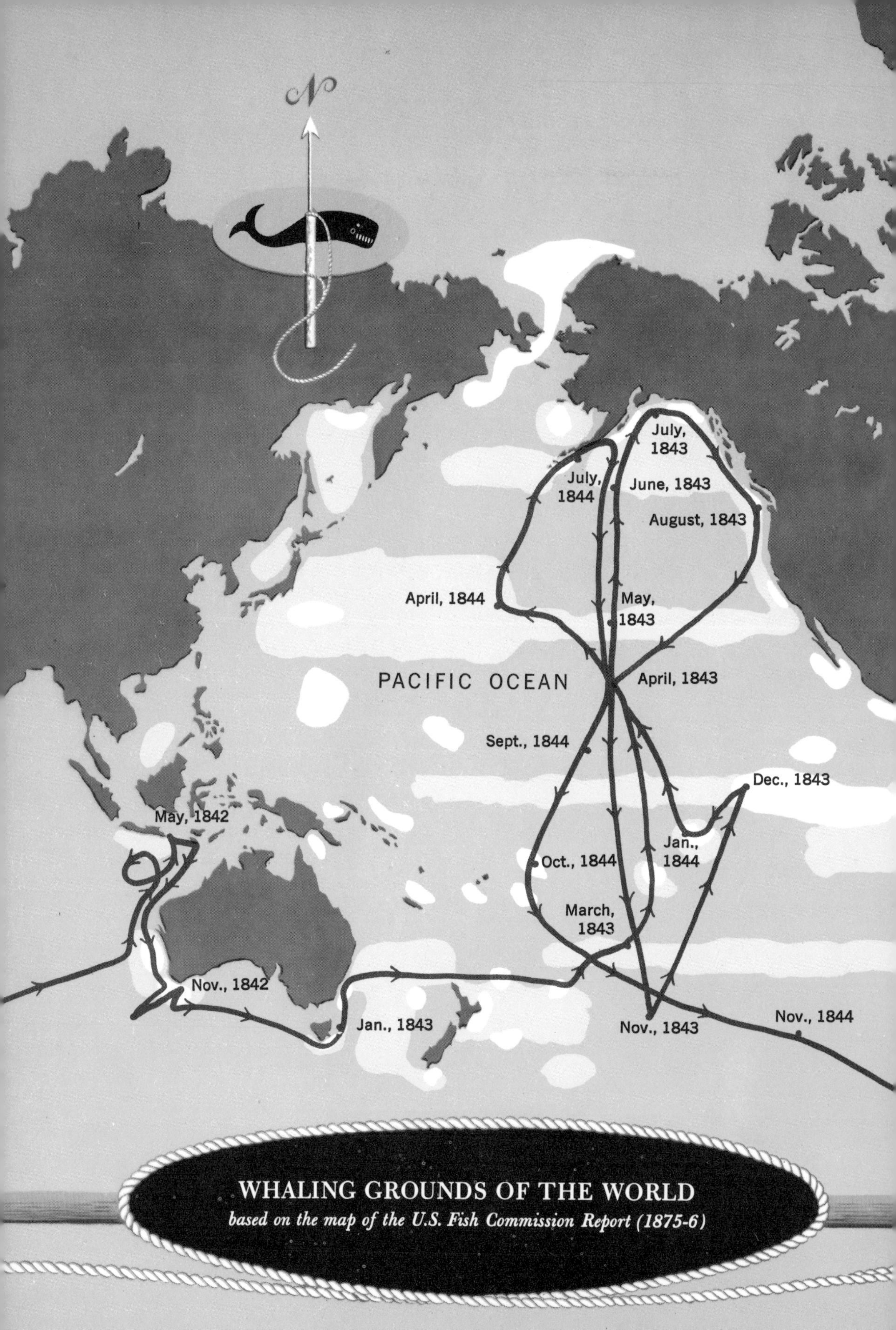

WHALING GROUNDS OF THE WORLD

based on the map of the U.S. Fish Commission Report (1875-6)

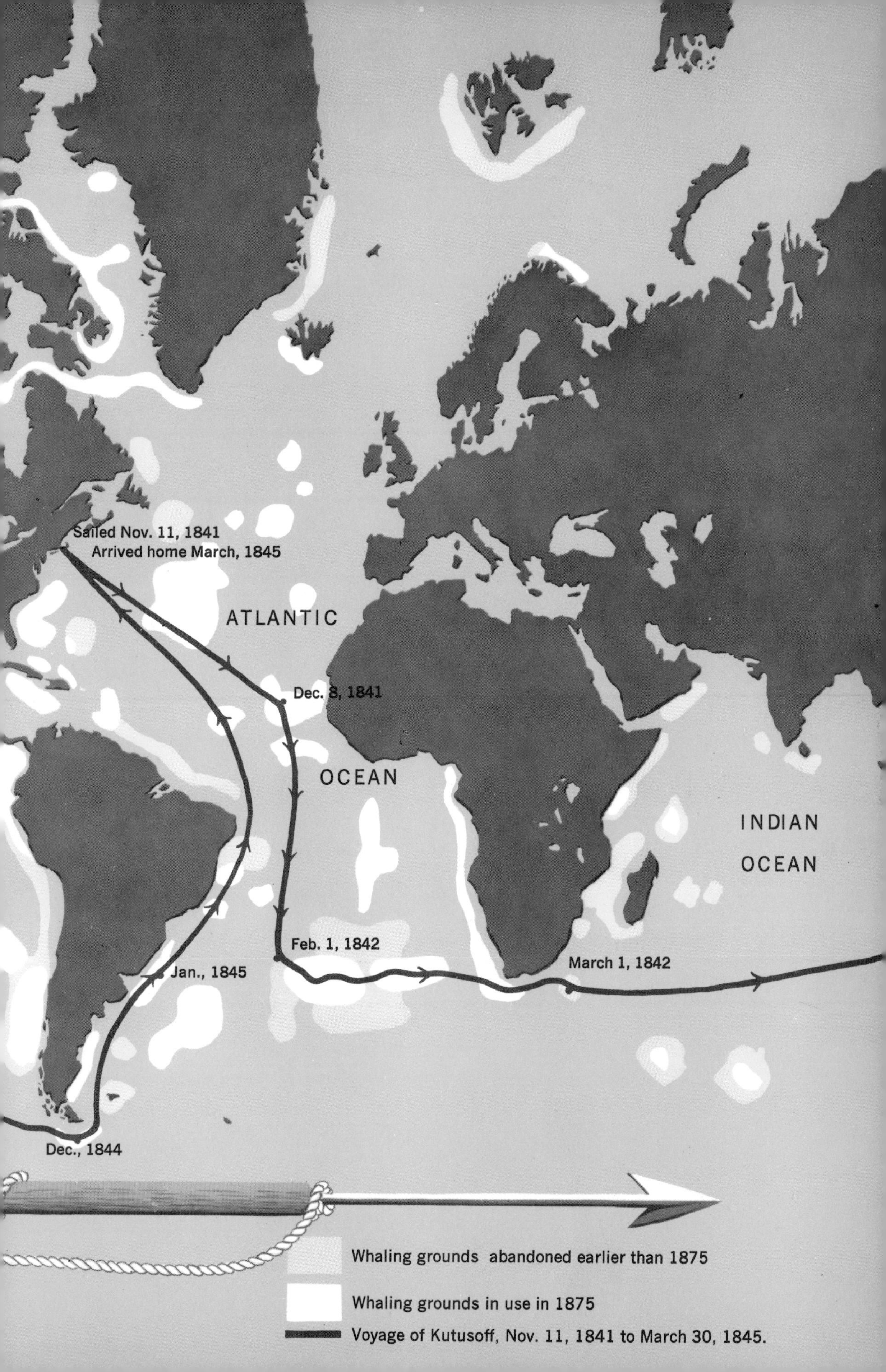
Sailed Nov. 11, 1841
Arrived home March, 1845
ATLANTIC
OCEAN
Dec. 8, 1841
Feb. 1, 1842
March 1, 1842
Jan., 1845
Dec., 1844
INDIAN
OCEAN
Whaling grounds abandoned earlier than 1875
Whaling grounds in use in 1875
Voyage of Kutusoff, Nov. 11, 1841 to March 30, 1845.

These pictures show the Arctic fleet disaster which occurred in September, 1871.

There was only one hope for escape—the five barks still in clear water a little to the south. The captains of all the vessels met and talked over the situation. Their food would last for no more than three months, and they could get neither food nor fuel from the land about them. It would be impossible for the crews to live here through the winter. They decided to abandon their ships, and to transfer the crews to the five barks.

On September fourteenth, captains and crews left their ships, making for the barks in their whaleboats. They took nothing with them except food and the most necessary clothing. About 1200 persons crowded into the five barks, and by October twenty-third they were safe in Honolulu. But the thirty-three ships, worth almost two million dollars, remained in the Arctic, their masts like dead sticks against a sky tortured by storms.

Five years later, twelve ships were caught in the ice, and fifty men lost their lives. In 1888, five ships sank in a storm off Point Barrow. In 1897, eight ships were trapped in the ice. George Fred Tilton, first mate of the *Belvedere*, traveled 3000 miles, much of it on foot, to get help.

American whalemen began to make voyages in steam whalers, and to kill whales with bombs and

Thirty-three vessels were trapped and crushed in the ice, but the crews were saved.

guns. They might have conquered the dangers of the Arctic. Indeed, in years to come, seamen of other countries would carry on Arctic whaling, using efficient factory ships and harpoons fired from cannon. It was not the Arctic itself that ruined American whaling. There were other reasons—mainly the scarcity of whales, and the lack of a good market for oil. But the losses in the Arctic helped to bring on the end, and the Yankee whaleman's final adventures came in the bitter waters of the North, surrounded by a fierce, frozen land.

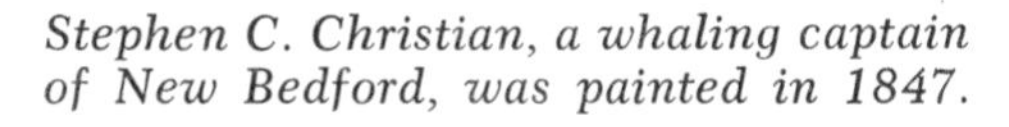

Stephen C. Christian, a whaling captain of New Bedford, was painted in 1847.

WHALING WIVES AND CHILDREN

Often, especially when whales were scarce, the days aboard a whaler could be slow and dreary. Still, there were always small tasks to pass the time, and scrimshaw. And at any moment whales might be sighted, and the cry of "There she blows!" would set off the excitements of another chase.

The days could be dreary, but night brought the hours of real loneliness. Darkness coiled around

Each of the ladies in this photograph was the wife of a New Bedford whaling captain.

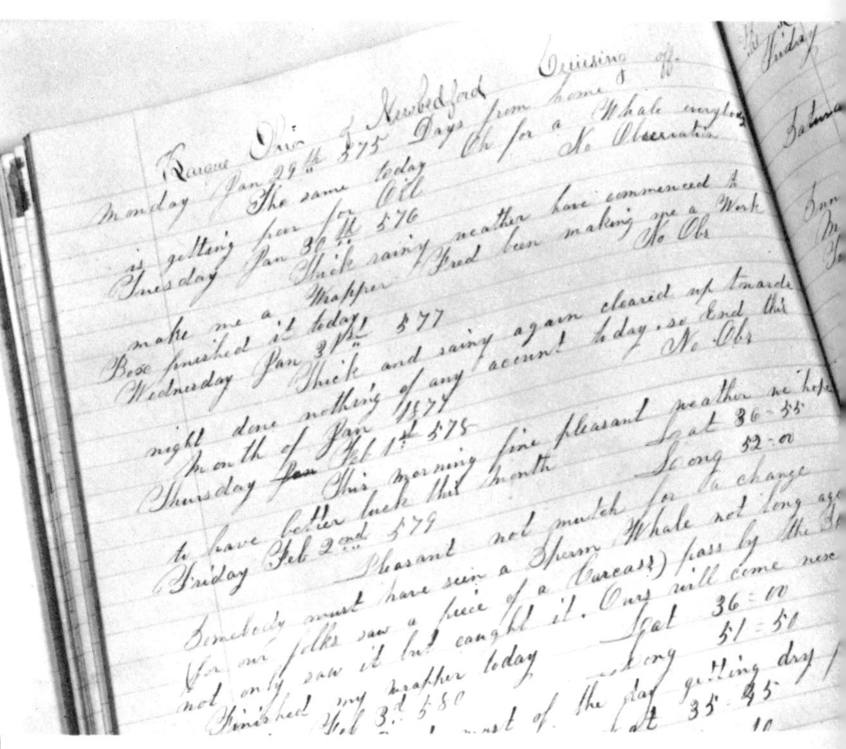

Barque Ohio of Newbedford Cruising off
Monday Jan 29th 575 Days from home
The same today Oh for a Whale anything
is getting poor for Oil No Observation
Tuesday Jan 30th 576
Thick rainy weather have commenced to
make me a Wrapper Fred been making me a Work
Box finished it today No Obs
Wednesday Jan 31st 577
Thick and rainy again cleared up towards
night done nothing of any account today, so end this
Month of Jan 1857 No Obs
Thursday Feb 1st 578
This morning fine pleasant weather we hope
to have better luck this month Lat 36-55
Long 52-00
Friday Feb 2nd 579
Pleasant not much for a change
Somebody must have seen a Sperm Whale not long ago
for our folks saw a piece of a Carcass) pass by the
not only saw it but caught it. Ours will come next
Finished my Wrapper today Lat 36:00
Long 51:50
Feb 3rd 580 most of the day getting dry
Lat 35 45

Mrs. Sallie Smith, who went on a whaling voyage on the bark Ohio during the years 1855 to 1858, wrote in her diary: "Fred been making me a Work Box . . . finished it today."

The "Fred" Mrs. Smith mentioned was her husband, Captain Frederick Smith. He built her the work box shown below, which was fitted out with scrimshaw clothespins made of whalebone.

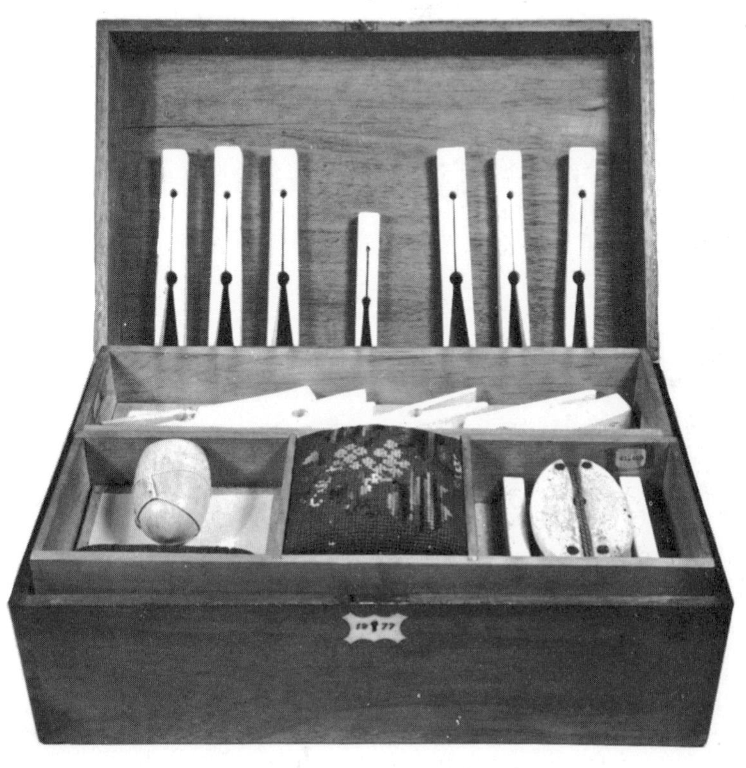

the ship like a sea serpent, held off only by the few whale-oil lamps burning below deck. The men who were not on watch sat or curled up on bunks as narrow as coffins. The lucky ones slept. Their lullaby was the creak and squeak of timbers, the whine of the wind, the wash and rumble of the waves.

These were the lonely hours when whalemen quarreled savagely over nothing, or made plans to desert, or whispered of mutiny. They stared at the shadows, feeling like orphan wanderers forever journeying to nowhere. What were they doing here? Why had they signed on this stinking blubber-hunter for three or four years of misery? They yearned for the land—their own land—for their own firesides, their own families, their own friends. They yearned for home.

It was in a night hour that one captain wrote, "O, what poor home-sick men . . . Home sweet home, and those we have left behind us are constantly on our minds. Little do those on shore know a sailor's feelings, separated from all that they hold dear on earth, with almost a certainty of being apart for three or four long years—enough to make a man's hair grow grey at the thought of it."

But there were those on shore who did know a sailor's feelings.

A pottery tray painted with view of Fayal, in the Azores. Wives sometimes stopped here to have their babies, while their husbands voyaged on to whaling grounds.

Dances by native women in the South Seas were often witnessed by whaling wives.

They were the wives of whalemen, and they had a loneliness of their own. In Nantucket, in New Bedford, or some other port town, they waited out the years that their husbands went whaling. At night, after the children were in bed and the whale-oil lamps lit, they could hear all the little noises of the house, and outside the howl of the sea-wind. This was the hour when they wrote letters, addressed to a man, a ship, an ocean, such as *Captain James Slocum, Bark Rainbow, Indian Ocean*, or *Bildad Smith, Whaleship Beaver, Pacific Ocean*. The letters were placed on outward-bound whalers, to be left at post boxes set up on islands like the Galápagos, where they could be picked up by the ships to which they were addressed.

In 1822, Mrs. Mary Hayden Russell, the wife of Captain Joseph Russell, decided that writing letters was not enough. With her young son, Charles, she left Nantucket and sailed to London. There she joined her husband on the whaler *Emily*. Her older son, William, was also on board, working as a boatsteerer.

And so Mrs. Russell became the first woman to go on a whaling voyage. She found living on a whaler much different from living in a house ashore. There was little space, for one thing. The bed took up most of the stateroom she shared with her husband. A bunk for Charles had to be made up on a sort of shelf above the horsehair sofa in the cabin, under the stern of the ship. At sea, Charles broke his arm.

"Such an accident on the land

Whalemen rowing to another ship for a gam, or a visit at sea.

would have been distressing," Mrs. Russell wrote in her diary, "but what were my feelings when I saw the child writhing in agony and no surgeon on board. . . . His dear father, with that fortitude and presence of mind that seldom forsakes him, took him below and, with a man to steady the arm, set it and splintered it up. The dear fellow bore the operation with courage that would have done credit to a man."

A storm came up, during which the cabin boy was swept overboard. Her older son William came to the stateroom and told her, "The hull of the ship seems to have not sustained any injury, but should it be otherwise and this night is to be our last, we will go trusting in the mercy of God." Although the sea "continued to rage with indescribable violence," the ship weathered the storm and all were safe—except for the lost cabin boy.

The first time the men lowered for whales, there was such a commotion that Mrs. Russell thought the ship was sinking. Then she stood at the rail, watching, while her husband and her son fought the monster whales. She wrote, "What a comfort at that moment to reflect that they were in the hands of God who was as willing as able to protect them. I could truly say: 'They that go down to the sea on ships, that do business in the mighty waters, they seeth wonderful works of the Lord.' "

Life on a whaler was sometimes hard to bear, but loneliness at home was worse, and many captains' wives followed Mrs. Russell's example. They were not always pleased with the company aboard ship. One wife said of the first mate,

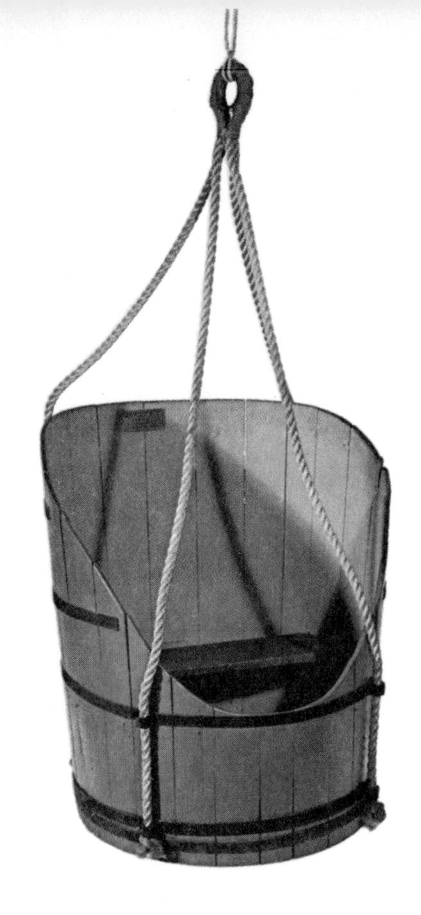

that would only hurry us. She is the meanest, most hoggish and greediest female that ever existed. Her looks is despised by everyone on board and the whistle of a gale of wind through the rigging is much more musical than . . . her voice."

But the crews of most "hen frigates," as whalemen called a ship carrying a woman, did not mind having the captain's wife

(*Continued on page 103*)

The gamming chair (left) of the bark Europa *was used to lower whaling captains' wives from ship to boat. A chair is shown (below) in a scene from the famous silent movie about New Bedford whaling, "Down to the Sea in Ships."*

"Without exception I think him nearest to a savage of anyone I ever met. He possesses a very quick, ungovernable temper, is also very jealous, and is very ignorant of the rules of good breeding, and yet has a very high opinion of himself. At times he is very social and at other times will not answer when spoken to. If we only had decently civil officers, I should enjoy life. As it is, there is but little enjoyment. All that induces me to endure it is my husband's society."

Nor were the officers always pleased with the wives. A mate on the whaler *Gazelle* wrote in his journal:

"Capt.'s wife got sick and so we made all sail for home. I wish she would have a sick time every day if

On a voyage of the whaler Roman, *which set sail from New Bedford in 1868, Captain Jared Jernegan (bottom right) took with him his wife Helen Clark (top right), his daughter Laura (left) and his son Prescott.*

MARCH 6. 1870.

MY DEAR GRANMA

WE ARE AT SEA NOW. I EXPECT WE
SHAL BE AT HONOLULU IN ONE WEEK
I HAVE A LITTLE KITTEN. SHE IS
GOOD. SHE IS BLACK AND WHITE.
I CAN WRITE A LITTLE. I AM GOING
TO HAVE A TEASET. PRESCOTT IS
OUT ON DECK. WHERE ARE YOU NOW.
I SHOULD LIKE TO KNOW WHERE.
I SUPPOSE YOU ARE IN EDGARTOWN.
I AM GOING TO WRITE AUNT EVA A
LETTER. YOU HAVE HAD TO WAIT
A LONG TIME FOR YOUR
LETTER. WE WENT TO AN ISLAND
NAMED OHITAHOO AND STAID
EIGHT DAYS. WE WENT TO THE
QUEENS PALACE. AND SHE MADE
A FEAST FOR US. MAMA WAS
THE FIRST WHITE WOMAN THAT
EVER WAS ON THE ISLAND. WE
HAD TEN DIFFERENT KINDS OF
FRUITES. I WILL NAME THEM.

While four-year-old Prescott played on deck, Mrs. Jernegan taught Laura her lessons. Laura was a good pupil, and at the age of eight wrote this letter to her grandmother who lived in Edgartown, on Martha's Vineyard.

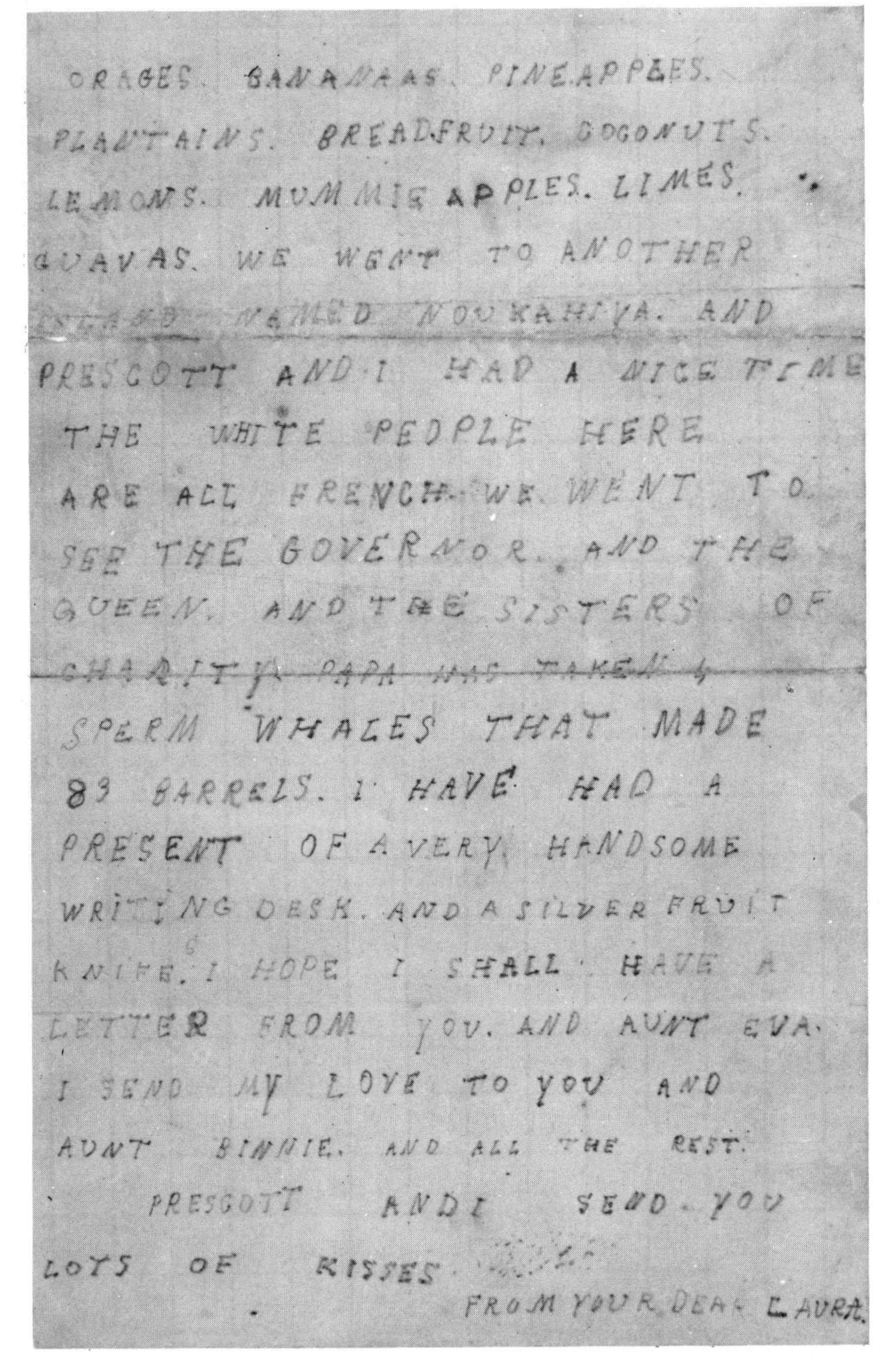

ORAGES. BANANAAS. PINEAPPLES.
PLANTAINS. BREADFRUIT. COCONUTS.
LEMONS. MUMMIE APPLES. LIMES.
GUAVAS. WE WENT TO ANOTHER
ISLAND NAMED NOUKAHIVA. AND
PRESCOTT AND I HAD A NICE TIME
THE WHITE PEOPLE HERE
ARE ALL FRENCH. WE WENT TO
SEE THE GOVERNOR. AND THE
QUEEN. AND THE SISTERS OF
CHARITY. PAPA HAS TAKEN 6
SPERM WHALES THAT MADE
83 BARRELS. I HAVE HAD A
PRESENT OF A VERY HANDSOME
WRITING DESK. AND A SILVER FRUIT
KNIFE. I HOPE I SHALL HAVE A
LETTER FROM YOU. AND AUNT EVA.
I SEND MY LOVE TO YOU AND
AUNT BINNIE. AND ALL THE REST.
PRESCOTT AND I SEND YOU
LOTS OF KISSES
FROM YOUR DEAR LAURA.

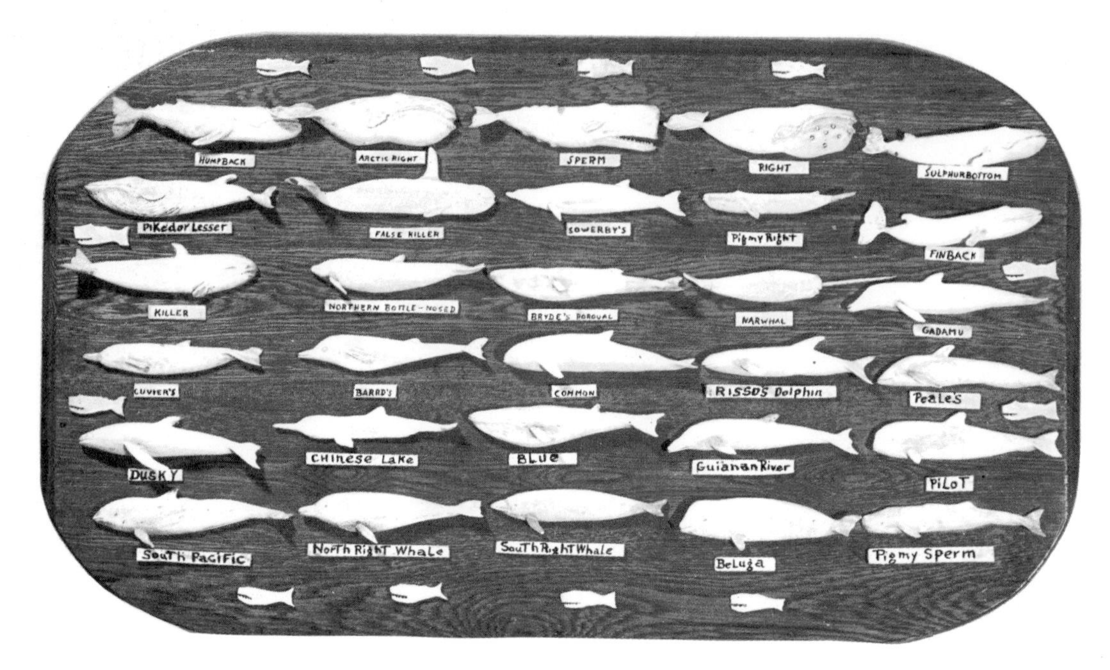

Scrimshaw was carved from the bones and teeth of whales, and sometimes from the tusks of walruses. Pictures and decorations were scratched on the surface and filled in with ink. Above is scrimshaw of various types of whales, mounted on a board. Below are a walrus tusk cribbage board (top), a decorated whale's tooth (left), a painted ivory plaque of whalebone (center), a jagging wheel or pie crimper (right), and a busk or stay (bottom), made of elastic whalebone or baleen, used to stiffen corsets.

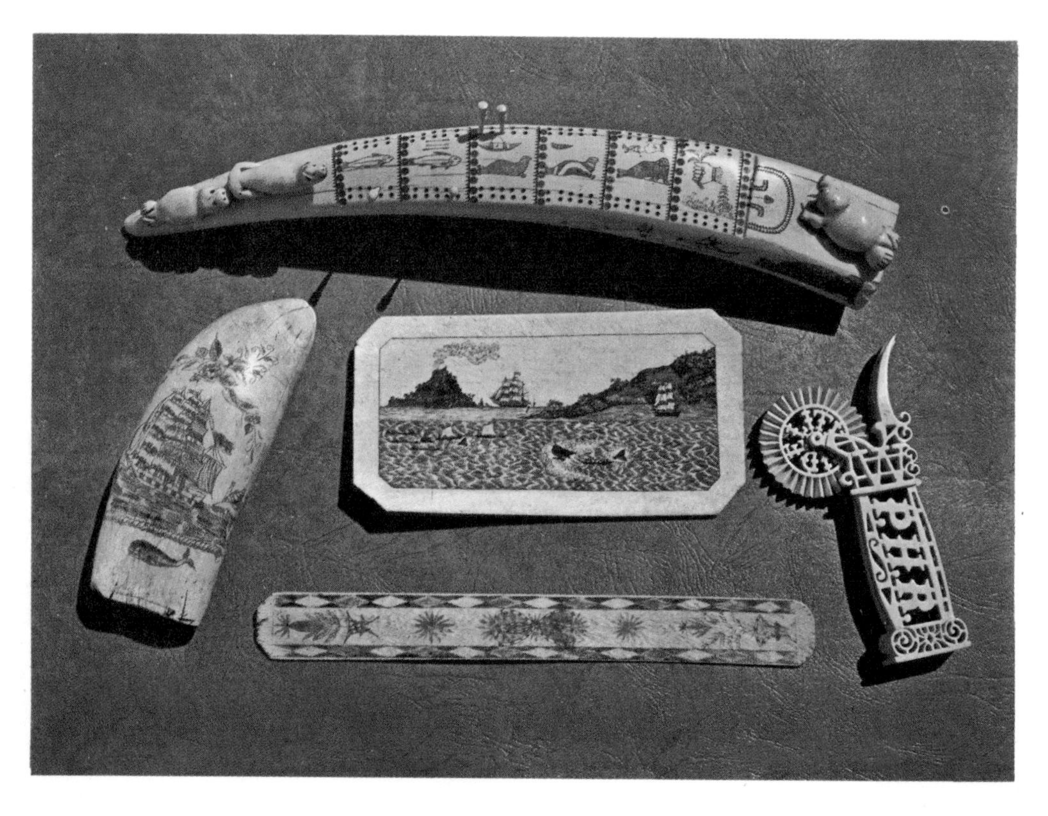

aboard. Sometimes they were even thankful. When eight men of the bark *Powhatan* came down with smallpox, they were doctored by the captain's wife, Caroline Mayhew. The captain caught the sickness, and she took over the navigation of the ship. After the captain was well, she herself became sick. She, too, recovered. In fact, as the captain said in a letter to the owners, "to my utter astonishment, we all got through without losing a man." The grateful crew loaded Mrs. Mayhew down with presents of scrimshaw—jagging wheels, swifts, knitting needles, and cleverly made boxes of ivory.

Other crews were grateful to Mrs. Charles A. Grant and to Mrs. Charity Norton, for different reasons. Mrs. Grant was on deck one day, hanging out her wash, when she spied the spout of a whale. Dropping her clothespins, she shouted, "There she blows!" The whale was a big one, and its oil filled many of the vessel's casks. The captain awarded her a silver dollar, which he usually gave to the first man to sight a whale.

Mrs. Norton was the wife of Captain John Oliver Norton, a hot-tempered man who was hard on his crews. She sailed with her husband on almost every voyage he made, and one whaleman said, "She had to, or he would never have come back alive." Time after time she calmed his temper and saved a sailor from punishment. In 1868, aboard the *Ionia*, twelve men tried to desert, and Captain Norton had them tied to the rigging.

"John, what are those men in the rigging for?" Mrs. Norton asked.

"I'm going to lick 'em. I'll give 'em a taste o' the cat," the captain said, meaning that he would beat them with the cat-o'-nine-tails.

"Oh, no, you're not," Mrs. Norton said, and the captain ordered the men set free.

The whaling wives made the hours pass by sewing and mending and washing clothes, by reading,

Crimper carved from whale's jawbone.

Jagging wheel used to seal pie crust.

Whalemen tying up whalebone, or baleen, the bony food strainers found in the mouths of several types of whales.

by writing diaries and teaching their children, and by battling cockroaches. A few had organs brought on board, and played music. They learned to know fog and calm and storm, and the look of death at sea: "After dinner I went below to lay down for a nap when I heard Daniel cry, 'Hard down the wheel! Hard down the wheel!' I ran up on the stairs to see what was the matter. It seems as though they were putting out a new sail and this colored man slipped and struck on the starboard boat. He never knew anything after he struck that boat. He went right down like a stone into the water. He must have broke his back or ribs. . . . It was a Terrible thing to think of a man being sent into Eternity without a minute's warning . . . ."

They went on gams, riding down to the water in gamming chairs. They saw strange sights, met strange people: "In all these places they have what they call a King, some places they have two. They have two in Salibaboo. We went to one of the King's houses. . . . After getting back aboard our vessel I began to cut out some work when one of the Kings and his wife came off to see me, so of course work had to be layed away and entertained

After a whale's jawbone was hauled up on deck, teeth were saved for scrimshaw.

Two carved, polished, decorated teeth of the sperm whale (above). The swift (below) was made of whalebone tied together with ribbons, and used for winding yarn.

The wooden sternboard of the whaler Mary and Susan, *beautifully carved and painted by an unknown craftsman.*

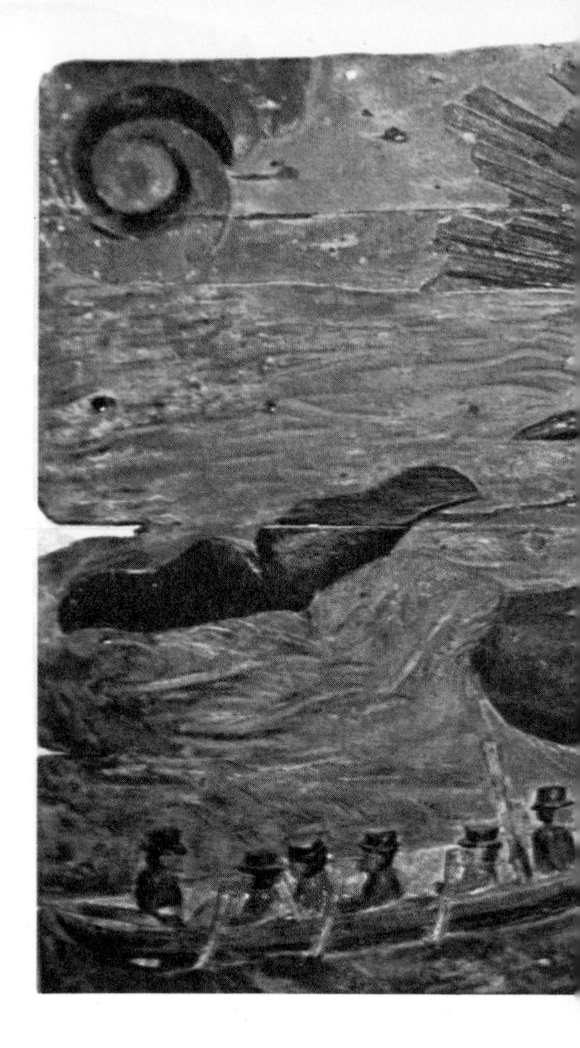

my company as best I could. I played on the Organ for them and it was amusing to see them stare at it to see where the sound came from. Then I showed them my stereoscope views which was a greater wonder to them than the organ. When they came aboard the queen brought me three baskets of beans and three of potatoes and a beautiful bird and three round baskets that they make on one of the Islands here."

And sometimes they remained on one of the strange islands, to bear their children. Or, while their husbands went whaling in the north, they stayed with the children for a while at places like Honolulu, beautiful places: "I kept wondering if I had died and gone to heaven. Numberless palms and tropical plants, and all hanging in a soft gleaming silvery sheen that went to my head like wine. . . ."

Some even knew mutiny: "The day we were going to sail, the sailors went on shore and when they returned to the ship had been drinking and refused to obey the order given by the mate. This was a mutiny. Seventeen men took three boats and left the ship, after nearly killing the mate and second officer. We were glad to see them leave the ship as I expected we would all be killed or that they would set fire to the ship. We left the harbor as soon as possible with a crew of only nine men and arrived in Honolulu in March, 1871."

The ship was the *Roman*, and the wife was Mrs. Helen Jernegan. Also on board were her two children, two-year-old Prescott, and six-year-old Laura. Laura kept her own journal of the voyage:

It is Sunday and a very pleasant day. I have read two story books. This is my journal.

Good Bye For To Day

We have had a gale two days. It is now moderate. We had corn

beans I am getting along with my lessons nicely.

Good Bye For To Day

Papa opened one of the coconuts. It is soft inside. Prescott loves them. There is a fly on my finger. He has flew of now.

Good Bye For To Day

it is a pleasant day, it is quite smooth to day. the men are boiling out the blubber in the try pots. the pots are real large. when the men are going to boil out the blubber, too men get in the pots and squis out the blubber and are way up to there knees of oil. . . . we had baked potatoes for supeper, and biscute. would you like to hear some news well I dont know of any.

Good Bye For To Day

And the children grew up, and some of the boys went whaling and some did not. And the girls married, and the captains' wives returned to Nantucket and New Bedford, to Edgartown and Sag Harbor. And all that remained of their voyages were the words in their journals, and some scrimshaw, and curiously formed shells that held the sound of the sea breaking on an island with two kings, where the sun shone on the palms waving in the delicious air.

WHALEMEN IN THREE WARS

Fighting against whales was war enough for most whalemen, but to make this kind of war they needed peace. They had no use for wars of men against men, which only interfered with whaling. And yet they were caught up in three such wars, and two whaling ships helped to bring about the American Revolution.

The two ships were the *Dartmouth* of New Bedford and the *Beaver* of Nantucket. After carrying a cargo of whale oil to London,

they were hired by the East India Company to carry tea back to America. On December 16, 1773, they were in Boston harbor, together with an English ship called the *Eleanor*. That night, American patriots held the Boston Tea Party. Disguised as Indians, they swarmed over the three ships and dumped the tea into the water.

It was one more step toward war between the colonies and Britain. When the fighting began in 1775, the whalemen hoped to keep out of it. Many of them were Quakers, whose religion forbade them to make war against men. Then, too, whaling was their only way of earning a living. But the war forced them off the seas and came to them on land. For, curiously, not one of the leading whaling towns escaped attack, by one side or the other.

Nantucket was raided by both sides. Hardly a month after the battles of Lexington and Concord, a strange ship tied up at the wharf. Marching to the racket of fife and drum, more than a hundred patriot soldiers tramped up the cobblestoned street into town. They had heard that some flour had been left here for General Gage, the British commander in Boston. For three days they searched the town and drank with Nantucketers in Pease's Tavern. They left without finding any flour, but they took with them fifty whaleboats.

The second raid, in April of 1779, was made by Tories who were still loyal to King George. They landed from seven vessels armed with cannon, and posted guards in the streets. The soldiers broke into stores and warehouses along the waterfront, loading $50,000 worth of goods on their ships. Angry but helpless, the Nantucketers watched them sail off with 260 casks of whale oil and hundreds of pounds

Two of the tea ships at the Boston Tea Party had once been Yankee whalers.

Lieut. Col. Return Jonathan Meigs.

of whalebone, iron, tobacco and coffee.

Sag Harbor had its battle in 1777. General Washington's retreat had left the British in control of Long Island. They used Sag Harbor as a supply center, building a small fort on the hill within the Old Burying Ground.

In May, a small American force under Lieutenant-Colonel Return Jonathan Meigs set out from Connecticut in thirteen whaleboats. They made their way to Sag Harbor, where they captured the commanding officer in his bed. They took prisoners and killed about six British soldiers in a charge on the fort. They set fire to a number of vessels, among them a schooner with twelve guns, and burned tons of hay, corn, oats and other supplies. At the end of twenty-five hours they were back in Connecticut with ninety prisoners. Not one American was lost. It was only a small action, but it came at a time when the Americans needed some cheering news.

All during the Revolution, the British were troubled by American privateers—private ships that had permission from the government to capture enemy vessels. In 1778 a British fleet set sail to attack any New England town that might have given shelter to privateers. On September fifth it struck at New Bedford. Not many able-bodied men

In the Revolution, the British captured Newport, Rhode Island, and used it as a naval base for attacks on American vessels and New England whaling towns.

were left in the little village; most had gone off to join the fighting in Rhode Island. The red-coated British soldiers marched through the town, burning about thirty vessels, as well as houses, warehouses, shops and supplies. In a few hours they destroyed about half a million dollars' worth of property.

Part of the British fleet went on to Martha's Vineyard. There was more burning and looting, and the people were forced to give up their sheep, cattle and firearms, and ten thousand pounds in cash. The British then started for Nantucket, where the islanders loaded their goods on carts and hid them in the hills beyond the town. But a wind came roaring up from the east, keeping the British ships at the Vineyard, and after a few days they were ordered back to New York. Nantucket was safe—until the Tory raid in April.

Although many Nantucketers remained loyal to the king, or simply took no side at all, others turned against Britain. They felt like Captain Nathan Folger, whose whaleship was captured by the British. Choosing to be imprisoned rather than fight on a British naval vessel, he said, "Hang me if you will to the yardarm of your ship, but do not ask me to be a traitor to my country!" Young Nantucket whalemen went privateering. Several were on the crew of the *Ranger*, under Captain John Paul Jones. And when

During the War of 1812, American seamen, like the one shown in this engraving, were captured and "impressed"—forced to work on British naval vessels.

Jones was given command of the *Bonhomme Richard*, most of the Nantucketers joined him—one of them, Reuben Chase, becoming a lieutenant.

For the seven years of the war, Nantucketers knew hardship and misery. Everything they needed had to be brought in by water. When they traded with British ports, they were stopped by American patriots and accused of smuggling. When they traded with American ports, the British took their ships. Nantucket whalemen were thrown into British prisons, or forced to work on British whalers, or to fight for Britain. Altogether, more than 1200 men were captured or killed, and 134 ships were seized. Food was scarce. There was a story told about a Nantucketer who tried to borrow a hammer.

"What do you want it for?" his neighbor asked.

"To knock out my teeth, I've got no further use for 'em."

During Revolutionary times, a number of families moved away. Some went to Nova Scotia. Others went to New York State, Maine, North Carolina, and to England and Wales and France.

As soon as the war was over, Nantucketers went back to whaling. In February of 1783, even before the peace treaty was signed, the ship *Bedford* arrived in London with a cargo of whale oil—the first ship to fly the American flag in a British port. One of the crew was a hunchback. Walking out on shore, he was slapped on the back by a British sailor.

"Ahoy, Jack," said the Englishman, "What have you got there?"

"Bunker Hill, and be damned to you," the American answered.

The United States and Britain fought again in the War of 1812, and again whalers were swept off the seas. Just as in the Revolution, the whaling towns knew hunger and hardship and fear. Children begged in the streets of Nantucket, and a soup kitchen was set up. Hundreds of whalemen were among the 6000 American prisoners held in prison in England.

As bad as the Revolution and the War of 1812 were for whaling, the Civil War was worse. By 1861 New Bedford had become the leading whaling port of the world. One day shortly after the war began, the whaling merchants there crowded into the banks and insurance offices on Water Street. A buzz and murmur of talk trembled in the air like the sound of trouble.

"No doubt about it. The *Atlantic* has gone down—sunk by a Confederate privateer."

"I was told the Rebs took off her crew and set her afire."

"That means none of our vessels is safe. If the Rebs keep it up, we'll all be ruined."

In two days, the merchants insured their ships for $1,000,000. The sum would have been larger, except that the insurance companies refused to sell any more insurance, even though they had raised the rates by fifteen per cent. Ships in port were kept tied up at the docks, next to old hulks that had not been to sea for years. Many ships that made port safely were not sent out again.

In October, government agents came calling at the counting rooms of the merchants. The Navy Department was buying up old ships. Weighted down with stone, they would be sunk at the channel entrances of Southern harbors to prevent blockade running into the ports of Charleston and Savannah.

Captains of the Stone Fleet—whalers sunk in Southern harbors in the Civil War.

The merchants were willing to sell, at prices from $3000 to $5000. Captains and small crews were hired. Carts rattled through the streets, hauling stone bought from farmers who had torn down walls on their land. Holes were bored into the hulls of the ships, fitted with plugs that could be pulled out to let in water.

On November twentieth, Thanksgiving Day, the first twenty-five ships of the "Stone Fleet" were ready. About half of them were from New Bedford, the rest from New London, Sag Harbor, Mystic, Nantucket, Edgartown. As the fleet set sail, signal guns were fired from shore. At Clark's Point a crowd watched, cheering and waving handkerchiefs. The guns, the cheers, the parade of ships, spread a feeling of holiday about the bay. But the people of New Bedford had little to be thankful for, this Thanksgiving. They were attending no celebration, but rather a funeral —and not only of the brave ships passing, but of whaling itself.

On December 20, 1861, they were sunk in the harbor at Charleston. On January 14, 1862, fourteen more ships were sunk. And the whole plan turned out to be useless. The tangled mass of wreckage settled deep into the bottom mud but failed to stop a single Confederate vessel.

The Stone Fleet was a sort of ghost fleet. Most of the ships, though still seaworthy, were old, and some were almost ancient. But there were still good, sturdy whalers at sea, hunting for whales. Now these began to go down, too, for in September of 1862 the Confederate cruiser *Alabama* went hunting for the whale-hunters. Built in England, she was a combination steam and sailing vessel, and carried eight guns.

First to be attacked was the *Ocmulgee*, a schooner from Edgartown on Martha's Vineyard. She was in the Atlantic, near the Azores, cutting in a big whale. It was a busy time, and the crew paid no attention to the ship coming toward them. Captain Abraham Osborne saw that she was flying the United States flag, and he thought she was a gunboat sent by the Union government to protect whalers. From her quarterdeck, her captain called to him through a speaking trumpet:

"I'm sending a boat on board of you!"

Before Captain Osborne could reply, a boat was lowered and came skimming toward the *Ocmulgee*. The boat's crew climbed up the side of the ship to the deck beside him.

Puzzled and angry, he burst out, "Who are you? What do you want?"

A young officer stepped forward. "You are a prize of the Confederate States Steamer *Alabama*, Captain

The Confederate cruiser Shenandoah *destroyed 29 whalers in the Arctic.*

Semmes commanding. Fetch your papers and come with us."

Captain Osborne's lean jaw tightened. The *Alabama* was lowering the United States flag and hoisting the Confederate flag in its place. And through her open ports he could see the hard iron mouths of her guns. As the young officer began to order him about, he said, "I don't care a cuss for you or your boat's crew. It's those guns that bother me."

He was taken aboard the *Alabama* and brought before her captain, Raphael Semmes.

"So you're from Edgartown," said Semmes, looking at Osborne's papers. "I thought so. You're the kind we are looking for. Anything from that blackhearted Republican town we must burn if it comes within reach."

"What will you do with my ship?"

"I am under orders from my government. There is only one thing I can do—take you and your men prisoners and destroy your ship. Pack your whaleboats with provisions and whatever else you may need, except your chronometer and your flag. Bring these to my cabin at once."

The Yankee whaleman stared at the Southerner, with his neat gray uniform, his white gloves, his pointed, waxed moustache. He had seen Semmes before. But where? And then he remembered. *At my father's house*, he thought, *having supper. Yes. . . .* Before the war, Semmes had come to the Vineyard to buy whale oil for government lighthouses, and had been a guest of the Osborne family. Osborne spoke of this to Semmes, but it made no difference. The whaler must burn.

Semmes had the crew of the *Ocmulgee* taken off, and at daybreak the next day she was set on fire. The oil-soaked ship blazed like a bonfire, dirtying the sky with black smoke. Her sides spilt; the oil in the hold had turned into a cargo of flame. Osborne watched, tears in his eyes, as the fire died down and the darkened hull dropped slowly beneath the water.

A little after ten o'clock that morning, Semmes brought the *Alabama* close to the island of Flores. He put off Osborne and his crew in their own whaleboats, and they made for shore.

Before they reached the island, the lookout of the *Alabama* sang

The sinking of the Stone Fleet, as shown in Leslie's Illustrated Newspaper, *in 1862.*

out: "Sail ho!" Semmes hauled down the Confederate flag, ran up the British flag, and went in chase of another Yankee whaler.

Altogether, until she herself was sunk off the coast of France by the U.S.S. *Kearsarge*, the *Alabama* sank, burned or captured seventy Union vessels. At least fourteen of them were whalers. Other whalers were destroyed by Confederate privateers. And in 1865, even after the war had ended, the cruiser *Shenandoah* destroyed almost the entire Arctic whaling fleet. Sailing up the Bering Straits, she burned twenty-four whalers within six days. Four more whalers were captured and used by the Confederates as transports.

Captain Raphael Semmes

The whaling industry never recovered from the loss of so many ships. This war of men against men helped put an end to the Yankee whalemen's war against whales.

Blockade plans failed, as the 45 vessels settled deep into the mud.

THE WRECK OF THE ESSEX

To a landsman, it might have seemed a nightmare. There was nothing, nothing at all but the immense sky, and the enormous sea like a desert of water. And under that immense sky, riding that enormous sea, was a ship.

She was the Nantucket whaler *Essex*. On November 20, 1820, she was in the Pacific, just below the equator. The nearest land was the Marquesas Islands, more than a thousand miles to the southwest.

The *Essex* carried twenty men—fourteen white, six Negro. To them, cruising this great stretch of open sea was no nightmare. It was simply part of their daily work, the work of whaling. Nor did the ocean seem to them an empty desert. They knew that whales came to these waters, and they were anxious for whales. They had left Nantucket a year and three months before, and they still had many casks to fill with oil.

Early that day, when the first light spread over the sky, three lookouts climbed to the mastheads. Around eight o'clock one of them sang out, "Blows! Ah blows!"

The crew came rushing out on deck, making a small stir and bustle on the enormous sea. Captain George Pollard called from the quarter-deck, "Where away?"

"Off the lee bow! There! There

Whales often stove in boats (as at right) but rarely did they ram a ship, as happened to the whaler Essex, *(above).*

blows! There blows another! Blows! There she blows and breaches! Looks like a school of 'em, sir!"

The ship bore down on the whales, and Captain Pollard spoke to the mates.

"Mr. Chase! Mr. Joy! Lower the boats! Pick out your own whales!"

The *Essex* had a good crew. Officers and seamen worked well together, and soon they had three boats in the water. One was commanded by the captain, the others by First Mate Owen Chase and Second Mate Matthew Joy. Chase's boat was the first to reach a whale.

"Steady, lads!" he whispered, for a loud noise might frighten off the monster. Chase was one of the few whalemen who handled both harpoon and lance. He changed places with the boat-steerer and stood in the bow, waiting for the right moment to attack.

He flung the harpoon, which struck deep and true. But he never got to use the lance. As the whale sounded, its flukes lashed out, knocking a hole in the side of the boat.

Chase cut the line with a few strokes of a hatchet, "Your jackets!" he said. "Off with 'em!"

An oarsman stuffed the jackets into the hole, to keep out the water until they could get back to the ship. And this, too, was no nightmare, but simply part of the day's work. A wounded whale would naturally thrash about, and a stove boat was nothing unexpected on a whaling voyage.

Luckily, the ship, which was being tended by the cooper, the cook, and the cabin boy, was not far off. Chase ordered the boat hoisted to the deck. He saw that it could be repaired with a piece of canvas nailed over the hole. If the men hurried, they might still catch a whale. They were hammering in the nails when Chase noticed something in the sea.

On the Galapagos Islands, whalemen capture turtles for fresh meat.

Lying quietly in the water was a huge whale, about eighty-five feet long. Its small eyes seemed to be watching them. It spouted, sank, rose again—and swam directly toward the ship.

"Put your helm up! Hard up!" Chase shouted to the boy at the wheel.

The ship swung about, but too slowly. A tremendous shudder ran through her, as though she had struck a rock. The men were thrown to the deck, and Chase grabbed at a ratline to keep from falling. They had been rammed by the whale.

Chase could hear water leaking into the hold. Ordering some of the men to start the pumps, he ran up a signal flag to call back the boats. The whale passed under the ship and lay at a little distance, watching. Suddenly, in a fit of madness, it beat the water with its flukes. Around it the sea boiled and churned. Rearing up from the foam, it clashed its jaws, as if raging at man for challenging its rule of the deep. The ship was settling. Chase and a few of the men ran aft to launch the spare whaleboats.

A voice cried from the deck, "He is making for us again!"

Its head half out of the water, its flukes whipping up a trail of foam, the whale charged the ship. With a crashing, tearing sound it smashed the bows. Then it dived, passed under the ship, swam off, and disappeared into the ocean.

A nightmare had begun for Chase and all on board. A stove boat was common enough, but never before had a whale destroyed a ship. The deck slanted as the hull filled with water; the vessel could not last long. Chase worked at the one undamaged boat, frantically trying to get it free.

"Steward!" he said. "Go to the cabin! Save what you can!"

The steward came back with two quadrants, two books on navigation, and two small trunks that belonged to the captain and the first mate. Chase managed to pick up two compasses. The men could feel the deck slipping away from their feet. There was no time to do anything but launch the boat. They were a length or two away from the ship when her masts tilted crazily through the bright air. Her sails drooped, and creaking and clanking, she toppled over on her beam ends.

The men stopped rowing. No one moved, no one spoke. They stared at the ship, wallowing in the waves. Only ten minutes ago they had been aboard a sturdy vessel, going about the business of whaling. It was impossible. Yet there lay the ship on its side, while they were in a small boat, and a thousand miles of sea between them and land.

The captain's boat glided up, followed by the second mate's. Captain Pollard stood at the stern, his face filled with such shock and amazement that he seemed a stranger. For him, too, a nightmare had begun. He stared at the dead ship, unable to say a word. At last, turning his head slowly, he spoke.

"My God, Mr. Chase, what is the matter?"

"We have been stove by a whale," said Chase, and explained what had happened.

Captain Pollard listened in silence, then had his boat drawn closer to the ship. They had been wrecked in a terrible and unexpected way, but they could not just

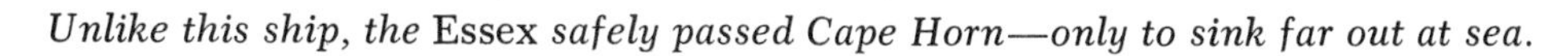
Unlike this ship, the Essex *safely passed Cape Horn—only to sink far out at sea.*

wait for death. They must try to save themselves, and they were seamen, and there were things they could do. At the captain's order, the men chopped off the masts of the ship, and she righted herself. Cutting holes in the deck, they took out from the hold two casks of bread, some casks of water, tools and compasses. They also found several live turtles they had picked up on the Galápagos Islands for fresh meat. They stayed with the ship for two days, strengthening their boats and rigging masts and sails.

The ship began to break up, and they decided to set off. But where should they go? Captain Pollard talked it over with his mates. Few ships had ever sailed this part of the Pacific, and there were no charts of these waters to guide them. If they went southwest, to the Marquesas, they might be killed and eaten by cannibals. If they went northwest, to the Sandwich Islands, they would surely run into hurricanes at this time of year. No, they had best go to the south and east, where the winds would carry them to South America. It was a 3000-mile voyage, and they should be able to make it in two months, before they ran out of food and water. Otherwise, their only hope was to find an island, or to be rescued by a whaler.

At noon of November 22, 1820, with the wind blowing hard and the waves high, they raised their sails. Six men were in First Mate Chase's boat; seven in each of the others, commanded by Captain Pollard and Second Mate Joy. They looked back at the hulk of the *Essex*, watching it until it disappeared in the distance. Then there was nothing, nothing at all but the immense sky, and the enormous sea like a desert of water. And under that immense sky, riding that enormous sea, were three small boats.

Each man was allowed only one biscuit of bread and a half-pint of water a day, and they soon began to feel hunger and thirst. They killed a turtle, drank the blood, and cooked the meat over a fire built in the shell. They fell on some flying fish that dropped into the boat and ate them raw. The hunger was bad, but even worse was the thirst. The sun blazed down, parching their throats, blistering their skins, burning out the juices of their bodies.

Storms came up, and lightning cracked the black sky. They lowered the sails and drifted with the huge waves. The boats leaked, and they bailed and repaired and patched. The wind died, and they rowed. They killed and ate another turtle. They scraped barnacles off the bottoms of the boats and ate them. For a month they sailed and rowed and drifted, until, on the twentieth of December, a man in Chase's boat called out, "There is land!"

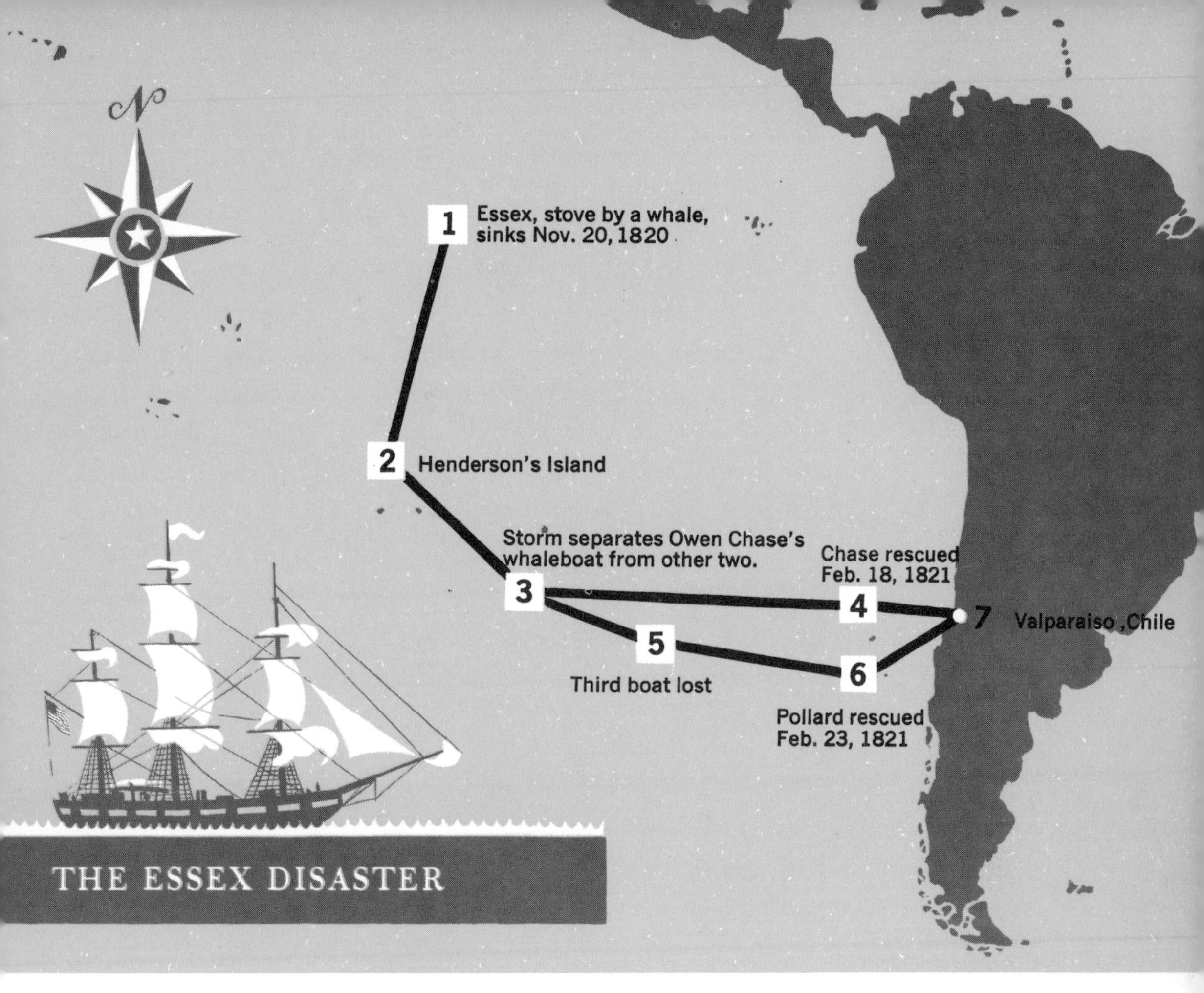

Map showing the routes of the survivors of the Essex *disaster.*

Before them, like something they had dreamed, lay a small island, where the waves broke gently on a white beach. Land! It meant water, food, shelter, rest—and it might mean cannibals. They found no cannibals. They did find a little food—birds, birds' eggs, crabs, fish—and water in a trickling spring. Within four days birds and eggs began to be scarce and crabs and fish were being frightened away. Twenty men could not live on this island. They would have to take to the boats again.

Captain Pollard made some calculations. He believed this place was Ducie Island. Winds and ocean currents had carried them far off their course, and again they had to decide which way to sail. They agreed to try for Easter Island, to the southeast, about 1200 miles away. Three men said they would stay here. The others repaired the boats, gathered birds and fish, and filled all the casks with water.

On December twenty-seventh, at six in the evening, seventeen men set off. By the following day, they were out of sight of land. Again there was nothing, nothing at all but the immense sky, and the enormous sea like a desert of water.

(*Continued on page 126*)

Benjamin Russell's panorama includes this imaginative scene of the whale ramming the Essex.

At first it was not too bad. They ate the birds and the fish, cooking them over fires built on stones they had brought from the island. Then they ran into a storm that carried them southward. The winds would never take them to Easter Island. Captain Pollard ordered the course set for Juan Fernández Island, 2000 miles to the east. The birds and fish had been eaten, and they went on rations of bread. Matthew Joy, the second mate, died. He was sewed up in his clothes, weighted down with one of the cooking stones, and lowered into the sea.

On the twelfth of January, a storm came roaring and howling out of the night. At every flash of lightning Chase looked for the other boats, but they were hidden by rain and waves. In the morning, when the sun shone again, they were gone. A sadness fell over Chase's men. From the moment they had left the wreck, they had tried to keep the boats together. There was something cheering and hopeful about the sight of the companions with whom they were sharing this nightmare. For a while they looked about, searching as far as they could. Then they gave up. There was nothing, nothing at all but the immense sky, and the enormous sea like a desert of water.

They sailed for nineteen days, and they were still 1600 miles from Juan Fernández. Chase cut their rations of bread to one and a half

ounces a day. They tried to kill a shark, but they did not have the strength to lance it. They tried to row away from a school of whales, but they were too weak to handle the oars. Richard Peterson, one of the Negroes, refused his bread, lay down, and quietly died. His body was lowered into the water.

They passed through storms and calms, calms and storms. By night, they huddled together, shivering with cold. By day, they tried to hide from the sun that seemed to turn the sea to flame. Boils and rashes broke out on their skin. Their lips swelled and cracked. When Chase slept, he dreamed of food, a nightmare within a nightmare.

On February eighth, Isaac Cole, one of the crew, quietly lay down.

"There is a great darkness in my mind," he said. "Everything is dark, all dark. No use to hope, Mr. Chase. We must die, and that is what I am going to do."

Chase pleaded with him not to give up, and Cole suddenly crept to the bows shouting, "You are right, Mr. Chase! I won't give up! I'll live! I'll live! I'll live as long as any of you! I'll live! Don't give up, lads! We'll all live!"

But he soon sat down again, quiet and lost in gloom. And the next morning he woke the boat, crying out, "I want my supper! And water! Water, there! And fetch me my napkin! My napkin, I say! A napkin for Cole! Where's my water? Where's my supper? Fetch me a napkin, blast you! Fetch it, I say!"

He had gone mad. The men covered him with old clothes, and he lay, groaning and shrieking, for hours. In the evening he had convulsions and died.

They let the body lie there through the night, and Chase could not sleep. Besides himself, there were Benjamin Lawrence and Thomas Nicholson, a boy of seventeen, left in the boat. They had bread for just three more days. Must they die, after coming so far? If only they had food, they would somehow reach land. Food . . . a bit

The crew of the Essex *feared cannibals such as these whom Captain James Cook witnessed making a human sacrifice.*

On long whaling voyages, fresh water was always a problem. In this panorama picture, casks are towed to shore on a South Sea island to be filled with water.

of meat . . . flesh. . . . In the thin starlight he could make out the body of Isaac Cole. There was food. Horrible—horrible to think about. But it would be even more horrible to die.

In the morning, Lawrence and Nicholson prepared to drop Cole's body into the sea. His voice low, Chase spoke to them about keeping the body for food. They quickly agreed. They separated the limbs from Cole's body, sewed up what was left in canvas and lowered it into the water. They roasted some of the flesh over a fire and put aside the rest.

Strengthened, although their arms and legs began to swell, they took turns steering the boat. Chase calculated that they were about 300 miles from land. A fresh wind blew up; perhaps it would carry them to safety. They kept watching the sails. The wind, the wind, the wind! It was their only hope, for the flesh was soon gone.

Chase dreamed he saw a ship in the distance, but no matter how he steered, he could not bring the boat closer. He awoke panting, sweating, almost crying with disappointment. Later he saw a heavy cloud settling on the water. Believing they were near land, he became more cheerful, and set a course for the cloud.

They were bailing out the boat the next morning, when Thomas Nicholson suddenly lay down. He pulled a piece of canvas over him and said he was going to die.

"No, no, Thomas!" Chase said. "It's only weakness, lad. You must not give up now. Trust in the Almighty to lead us to safety."

The boy looked at him coldly and after a while, Chase stopped talking. Feeling weak and dizzy himself, he fell asleep. He was awakened by a shout from Benjamin Lawrence:

"There's a sail!"

Chase stood up. Thomas threw off his canvas covering and jumped to

his feet. Smiling, shaking with excitement, their clothes in rags, they looked like three jolly, bearded skeletons as they steered toward the ship. She was the brig *Indian* of London. They were too weak to climb up the side, and had to be carried up by some of the ship's crew.

It was February 18, 1821. Since leaving the island, they had been at sea for 53 days and had traveled 2200 miles. They had traveled 3700 miles since leaving the wreck. A week later, they arrived in Valparaíso, on the coast of Chile. And two weeks after that the Nantucket whaler *Dauphin* made the same port, carrying Captain Pollard and young Charles Ramsdell.

The five men of the *Essex* met and told their stories. Chase had left behind two boats, one commanded by the captain, the other by Third Mate Obed Hendricks. They, too, were soon without food. As one man after another died, his flesh was eaten by those who remained alive.

On January 28, 1821, the two boats were separated in a storm, and Hendricks' boat was lost forever. With Captain Pollard were his nephew, Owen Coffin, the young

Herman Melville's novel, Moby Dick, *was partly inspired by the story of the* Essex. *Rockwell Kent's drawing shows the monstrous white whale breaching.*

cabin boy; Charles Ramsdell, who was not much older than Coffin; and Barzillai Ray. Two men, two boys—and not a crumb of bread, not a scrap of raw fish to eat. One of them had to die, to furnish food for the rest. Facing each other in the little boat, on the enormous sea, they drew lots. To Owen Coffin fell the lot that meant death.

Captain Pollard stared at his nephew in silence. Then, starting forward, he harshly cried out, "My lad, if you don't like your lot, I'll shoot the first man that touches you!"

"I like it as well as any other," Owen Coffin said.

"Let me take your place, lad," the captain said, but the boy would not listen.

With trembling hands, the captain, Charles Ramsdell and Barzillai Ray drew lots again, to see who would do the killing. This time the lot fell to Ramsdell.

"Look!" he said. "I will go in your place, Owen! Let me die instead!"

"No," Owen Coffin said, "it is my right to die."

And he lay his head on the gunwale, holding it so that the bullet would not pierce the boat. Captain Pollard gave Ramsdell his pistol and turned away. Long after the shot was fired, it seemed to roar and echo like thunder. But they prepared the body for food, for there was nothing else they could do.

Less than two weeks later, Barzillai Ray died, and his body was also used for food. So Captain Pollard and Charles Ramsdell remained alive, and on February twenty-third they were rescued by the *Dauphin*.

An arrangement was made with the *Surrey*, an English ship bound for Australia, to pick up the three men still on the island. It proved to be Henderson Island, rather than Ducie Island, and there the *Surrey* found the three men. They had been waiting for 102 days.

The five Nantucketers returned to their homes, but the nightmare would never be over. They carried it with them in the hollows of their skulls. The memory of its horrors—the heat, the hunger, the thirst, the dying, the taste of human flesh—would rise and burn their brains like a fever. So they said little about it, even to their families and friends, and tried to forget, and they forgot enough to go back to sea.

Chase, Lawrence, Ramsdell and Nicholson became captains, commanding their own ships. Captain Pollard sailed to the Pacific on the whaler *Two Brothers*. The ship struck a coral reef and was lost, but Captain Pollard was rescued after a few days.

"Now I am utterly ruined," he said. "No one will ever trust me with a whaler again, for all will say I am an unlucky man."

He gave up the sea, and took a job as one of the town watchmen of Nantucket. For forty years he walked the dark streets at night, carrying a nightmare in his skull. The five Nantucketers who had been on the *Essex* grew old, and one by one they died—Ramsdell in 1866, Chase in 1869, Pollard in 1870, Lawrence in 1879, and Nicholson in 1883.

Their sons and daughters tried to let the nightmare die, too. Even years later, one of them listened to a friend's question about the shipwreck, then answered:

"Miss Mollie, here we never mention the *Essex*."

But the nightmare was not over, for the whaling captains never tired of talking about it. They wondered whether Captain Pollard should not have taken his boats to the Marquesas, and risked trouble with the savages. Or perhaps he should have gone to Pitcairn Island, or the Society Islands, or to the Sandwich Islands, where there was no hurricane season. In the end they always recalled that Captain Pollard had been in unexplored and uncharted waters, and that his seamanship could not be doubted.

And tales were told, in the town and beyond it. Some were true, like the one about Owen Chase. As an old man, a retired whaling captain, he still feared hunger. He bought more food than he needed and hid crackers in the attic of his house.

And so in tales, in talk, in books, in old documents, the nightmare remained. And it would go on, while men still told the story that began with nothing, nothing at all but the immense sky, and the enormous sea like a desert of water. And under that immense sky, riding that enormous sea, was a ship—a ship that was sunk by a whale.

MUTINEER'S KINGDOM

The Young Mutineer, the Terrible Mutineer, were the names the whalemen gave him. That was after they had heard of the blood and horrors at midnight, of the massacre on a sandy shore, of bones crumbling under a lonely rock.

His real name was Samuel Comstock. He was born a Quaker, but his ways were never Quaker ways. Even as a boy on Nantucket he had his secrets. He roamed the island from morning to night, and where or why he went no one could say. When he got into trouble—and he got into trouble often, because he was fearless and hated rules—he

The Globe *mutineers hid on an island like this one, pictured in Russell's panorama.*

was quick to make up excuses. He was just as quick to give promises. Once, refusing to take his small brother roaming with him, he promised to bring back forty little kegs of molasses bound with bright golden hoops.

He was sent away to several schools, but no school could hold him. For there was a power in Samuel Comstock. It was a strange power he did not understand. He knew only that it would not let him rest, driving him to do whatever was daring or forbidden. His family moved to New York City, and he led the Downtown Boys in gang fights against the Corlear's Hookers. He came home with great gashes on his arms and legs, which left scars that never disappeared.

At the age of thirteen, he ran away to Philadelphia, to go to sea. He was brought back, and his father arranged for him to ship out on a merchant vessel. By the time he was nineteen, he had made two whaling voyages and was a boatsteerer. Returning home, bold, reckless, boastful, he shocked his father's Quaker friends. He enjoyed shocking people. And yet women loved the strutting young whaleman with the cruel eyes, and men saw something in him they admired and feared.

He decided to become an officer on a naval frigate, and his father agreed to pay for his outfit. The Quakers persuaded his father not to give him the money to sail on a ship of war, and he went off on another whaling voyage.

He seemed to go willingly enough. And this was strange, because he did not care much for whaling. But a terrible anger was building up in Samuel Comstock. At last he understood his power. He was not like other men and could not live by their rules. He was meant to command, not to obey. He would have a kingdom of his own, to rule as he pleased—and he had a plan to get it. He would take over the ship, kill off the crew, and set himself up as king of the natives of some Pacific island. From his island kingdom he would raid ships on the South Seas. All the world would know the name of Samuel Comstock and tremble before his power.

And so it was that in December of 1822 the whaler *Globe* of Nantucket sailed with a whaleman who wanted to be a king. Comstock hated the officers, who stood between him and his kingdom. Every order they gave him fed his anger and made him eager for revenge.

He studied his shipmates, wondering which to recruit for his mutiny. As the weeks passed, they grumbled about the strictness of Captain Worth and complained about the food. Comstock talked to them slyly. When the ship touched at Oahu, in the Sandwich Islands, six men deserted and were replaced by six others. They were shiftless, homeless wanderers, and Comstock knew that among them he would find his recruits.

On January 26, 1824, he was ready to strike. That day began with blood. Joseph Thomas, one of the new hands, was slow to obey the captain's orders and talked back to him sneeringly. Captain Worth whipped him with a rope.

The *Globe* was having a gam with the *Lyra* of New Bedford, and they were traveling in company for a while. At night a fog rose from the sea. Drifting silently on the heated air, it spread between the two ships.

Aboard the *Globe*, Samuel Comstock's younger brother, George, was at the wheel. George was fifteen years old and on his first voyage. He peered through the darkness, but he could see little beyond the glow of the binnacle—the stand before him that held compasses and a lamp. Floating out of the fog, the hundred small noises of the ship seemed suddenly important. And among these noises were whispers spoken by men.

George tightened his grip on the wheel. Had he really heard anything? He could not be sure. He had been on watch for almost two hours and he was tired. At midnight he picked up the rattle kept near the binnacle. Its noise would signal the next man scheduled for duty to take over the wheel. But before he could shake the rattle, a voice from the darkness stopped him. Stepping into the glow of the binnacle, Samuel Comstock said:

"Make the least damned bit of noise, and I'll send you to hell."

He put down the knife he was carrying and lit a lantern from the binnacle lamp. He was joined by three of the new hands. They were Silas Payne, John Oliver, and

Mutinies were not uncommon on whalers. Russell's painting shows the 1842 mutiny on the Sharon, *staged by native crewmen signed on at Hawaii.*

William Humphries, the Negro steward. Humphries took the lantern. Payne had a knife and an axe, and he gave the axe to Comstock. Moving as quietly as the fog, they all went down the companionway to the officers' cabin below.

For a few minutes the only sound was the small noises of the ship. Then from the cabin came the crash of an axe against flesh and bone. There was a scuffling, a thudding, a pounding of blows, and a long, loud scream. Gilbert Smith, another boatsteerer, ran across the deck to the companionway. He stared down into the cabin, gasped, and ran forward to the forecastle. Samuel Comstock's attempt to win a kingdom had begun.

Comstock came plunging out on deck, carrying the unlit lantern. His eyes were wild, and his hands, his arms, his face, and his torn shirt were spattered with blood. He brought the lantern to the binnacle to light it again, and George asked, "Are—are you going to hurt Smith?"

"Yes. I'm going to kill him. Have you seen him?"

"No. No. I don't know where he is . . ." George's voice broke and tears streamed from his eyes.

Comstock glared at him. "What are you crying about?"

"I'm afraid they'll hurt me."

"*I'll* hurt you if you talk in that manner!"

He hurried down the companionway again. There was more scuffling and pounding, followed by the blasts of a musket, and Comstock's voice shrieking:

"I am a bloody man! I have a bloody hand! I will be avenged!"

Bursting from the companionway, Comstock stamped about like a madman. He called for Smith and asked if he would join the mutineers.

His face white with fear, Smith answered, "I will do anything you tell me to."

A lantern was hoisted as a signal to the *Lyra*. Both ships were to tack—swing off in another direction—at the same time. Comstock ordered that the *Globe* stay on course. The *Lyra* would tack, and the two ships would draw apart.

Quickly the bodies of the captain and the three mates were hauled up on deck and heaved overboard. Second Mate Lumbard had been stabbed several times with a bayonet, and his body leaked blood. But as he was dropped over the side, he caught hold of the edge of the deck and hung on.

"Comstock!" he cried, in a thin, wheezing wail. "Comstock . . . you said you would save me!"

Comstock stamped on the mate's

Map of the route of the mutineers from the whaler, Globe.

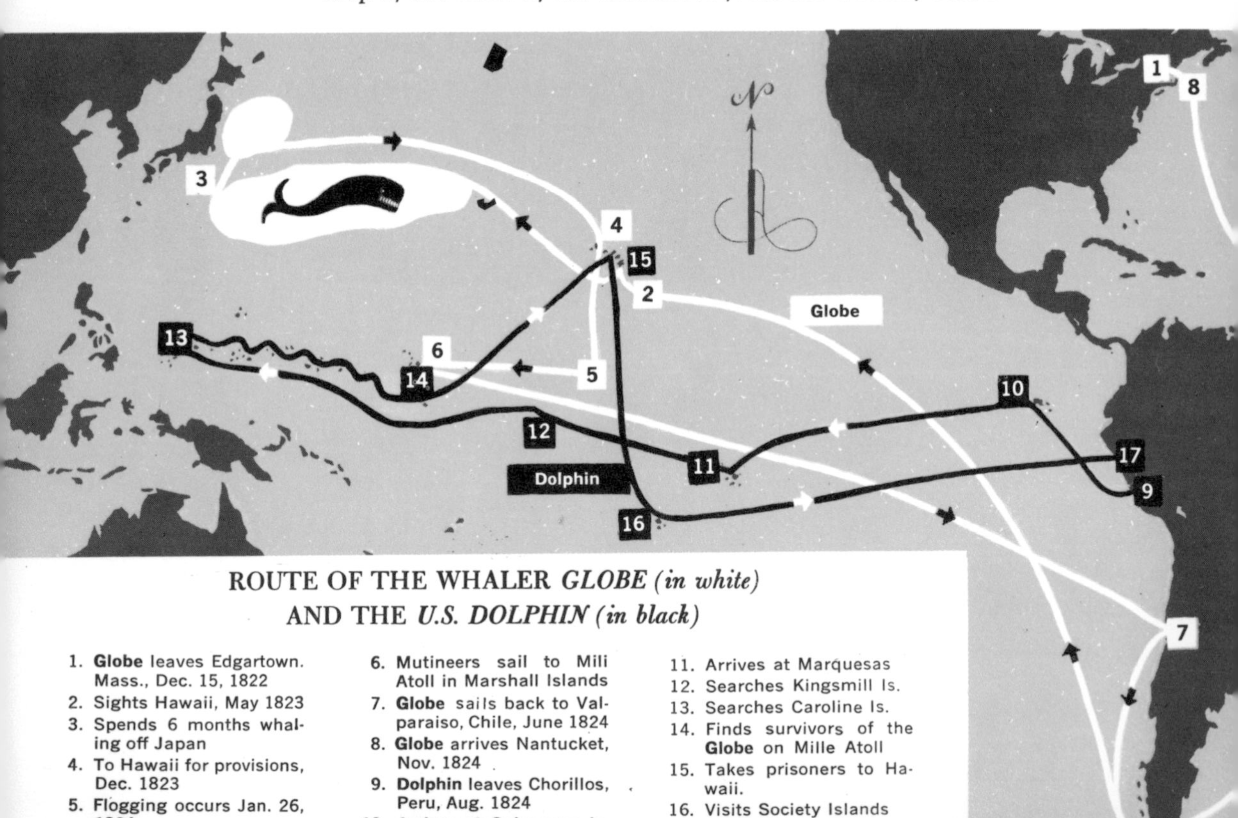

fingers with his heavy boots, crushing the bones until Lumbard slid down into the sea. And still the man would not die. The crew heard him splashing in the darkness, trying to swim. Comstock shrugged. The sharks would finish him off.

Comstock named Payne as his mate, and ordered the crew to throw overboard all the whaling gear and equipment—except the try-pots. The *Globe* was no longer a whaler. She was Comstock's ship, a royal ship that would carry him to his kingdom. He laid down new laws for the crew. If any man saw a vessel and did not report it, or refused to fight a vessel, he would be put to death by boiling in a try-pot of oil.

A few days after the mutiny, Humphries was found loading a pistol. Comstock put him on trial before a jury of four men, who found him guilty of loading a pistol so that he could shoot down Comstock and Payne. A cap was pulled over Humphries' face. A rope was put around his neck and run through a block on the fore-yard. Comstock ordered every man on board to take hold of the rope and pull when he gave the signal on the ship's bell.

"You have fourteen seconds to live," Comstock told Humphries.

Humphries said quietly, "When I was born, little did I know I should ever come to this. . . ."

The Globe, *off the Marshall Islands. This picture (and those on pages 140–141) are taken from* The Life of Samuel Comstock, the Terrible Whaleman, *written by his brother William Comstock in 1840.*

The bell rang, the men pulled, and Humphries swung out over the sea. He died at once, without even a kick or a groan.

Across the Pacific, searching for his secret kingdom, Comstock guided the ship. He told no one his plans. Suspicious of the men, who could so easily turn against him, he watched them carefully. But within himself he felt a fierce joy nothing could spoil. Payne and Oliver often woke at night, haunted by dreadful dreams of the men they had murdered. Comstock laughed. He, too, had dreams. Once he had seen Captain Worth pointing at his bloody head.

"I told him to go away," Comstock said. "And I told him if he ever appeared again, I would kill him a second time!"

And, indeed, Comstock had not finished with killing. Stopping at an island to pick up fresh food, he ordered the crew to fire at some natives who tried to steal a few small things from the ship. At least one native was killed.

In the second week of February, after sailing about a thousand miles, Comstock brought the ship to the Mille Atoll, in the Marshall Islands. The natives, who wore only loincloths and sashes, laughed at the queer clothes of the strangers. But they were friendly, and Comstock decided that here he would establish his kingdom.

Leaving Payne in charge of the ship, he set up his headquarters on the island—a tent made of a spare sail. Then he had the crew build rafts and bring all the equipment of the ship on shore. This was something usually done by mutineers before they burned the ship they had captured. But Payne became suspicious when he saw that Comstock was giving many of their supplies to the natives. He was trying to win the friendship of the natives. For what? So that they would attack the men of the *Globe* and leave him to rule the island? Payne made his way to Comstock's tent. In the hot, white light filtering through the canvas, the two mutineers faced each other and had a savage quarrel.

It ended with Comstock shouting, "I took the ship, and have navi-

Tahitian natives shown here lived much like those who killed the Globe *mutineers.*

gated her to this place. I have also done all I could to get the sails and rigging on shore, and now you may do what you please with her. But if any man wants anything of me, I'll take a musket to him."

Comstock went to the ship and picked up the captain's cutlass.

"I am going to leave you," he said to the crew. "Look out for yourselves."

In the evening, Payne saw Comstock and a crowd of natives walking toward the little village of thatched huts under the cocoanut palms. Had Comstock given the natives any of the ship's muskets? If he had, they might attack at any time. Payne posted sentries around the tent, and they waited. All night they waited. And in the morning, as the sun rose, a sentry cried out, "Here comes Comstock!"

Arming themselves with muskets, Payne, Oliver, and two other men knelt on the ground. Comstock came toward the tent. Then he stopped, looked up, and saw the four men. He drew out his cutlass, took another step, and stopped again.

"Don't fire!" he said. "I haven't come to hurt you."

"Fire!" said Payne.

There were four blasts of flame from the muskets, and Comstock fell forward to the sand. Dropping his musket, Payne brought an axe down hard on Comstock's head.

Payne called all the men together and ordered them to dig a grave, on the beach near a large black rock. Comstock's body was sewn up in a piece of canvas and put in the grave with the cutlass beside it. Payne asked Gilbert Smith to read something from the Bible. Standing beside the rock, Smith opened the book to the fourteenth chapter of Isaiah. While the sea beat against the glistening shore, while the wind moved gently in the palm trees, he read:

A flogging set off the Globe *mutiny.*

"How art thou fallen from heaven, O Lucifer, son of the morning! . . . For thou hast said in thine heart, I will ascend into heaven, I will exalt my throne above the stars of God. . . . Yet thou shalt be brought down to hell, to the sides of the pit. . . ."

Sand was shoveled into the grave, a musket was fired, and the men turned away. Comstock's kingdom was fallen, gone with the mutineer who wanted to be king.

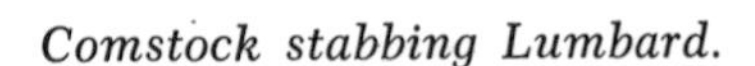
Comstock stabbing Lumbard.

But not quite. The king was dead, and Payne had to take his place as ruler of the mutiny and the island. And Payne did not like being a ruler. Most of the men had not taken part in the mutiny and were here against their will. They could rise up against him, or even sail off on the *Globe*. Before the day was over, he ordered that the *Globe's* two binnacle compasses be brought to him. Without a compass, the men could never find their way across the sea.

Payne was not enough of a whaleman to know that there was

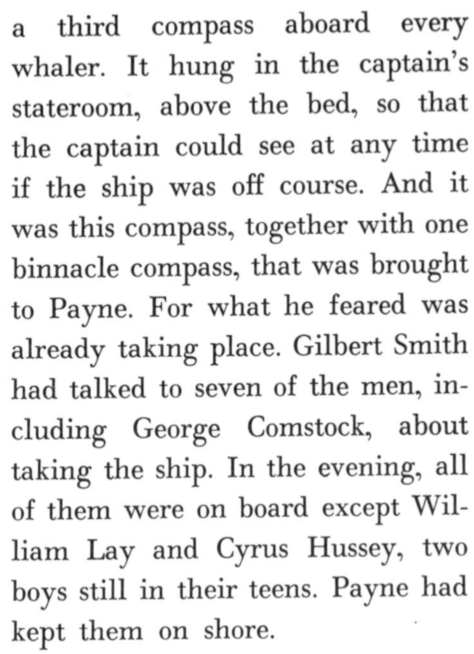
a third compass aboard every whaler. It hung in the captain's stateroom, above the bed, so that the captain could see at any time if the ship was off course. And it was this compass, together with one binnacle compass, that was brought to Payne. For what he feared was already taking place. Gilbert Smith had talked to seven of the men, including George Comstock, about taking the ship. In the evening, all of them were on board except William Lay and Cyrus Hussey, two boys still in their teens. Payne had kept them on shore.

The moon rose around nine-thirty, and the men saw it would be dangerous to wait any longer for the two boys. They cut the ropes that held back the ship, and in the moonlight, as silently as they could, they sailed away, leaving behind what was left of Comstock's kingdom.

On June 7, 1824, they arrived in Valparaíso, Chile. The American consul there arranged for the *Globe* to sail home, and before the end of November she was back in Nantucket.

When Samuel Comstock's father was told the news, he thought of his son, the bloody man with the

The execution of Humphries.

bloody hands, buried under a rock on a lonely island.

"Oh, Samuel, Samuel!" he said. "Heaven-forsaken Samuel!"

The whaling merchants, too, thought of Samuel Comstock, but they thought of other things as well—of their ships on far waters, of their rich cargoes of oil, of crews that might take a notion to mutiny. The *Globe* mutiny was one of the worst in the history of whaling, and they did not want it repeated. They wrote letters to Washington, asking the government to find and punish the mutineers still on the island. And so, on August 18, 1825, the United States schooner *Dolphin* set out from a port in Peru to find Comstock's lost kingdom—and the lost mutineers. They searched for months, until, in the Mille Atoll, they found a place strewn with barrel staves, pieces of canvas, bits of rigging. A little distance away, there was a skeleton in the sand and a box with a few Spanish dollars. Captain John Percival of the *Dolphin* sent eleven men under Lieutenant Hiram Paulding out in a launch to cruise the islands.

On one of them, Lieutenant Paulding saw a large gathering of natives. Anchoring his boat, he stared at the crowd, and at the huts in a grove of palm trees. Suddenly a man stepped out from the crowd and called to him in English: "They are going to kill you. Don't come on shore unless you are prepared to fight."

The man wore nothing but a mat around his loins. His skin, glistening with cocoanut oil, had been burned by the sun until it was almost as dark as the natives'. And, like the natives', his hair was long and tied in a knot on top of his head.

"Don't come ashore," he said. "They think I am getting you to land, so they can attack you with stones."

"What is your name?" Paulding asked.

"William Lay of the *Globe*, of Nantucket."

"Come to the boat!" Paulding said. "Make a run for it. We'll protect you."

"No, they would kill me with stones before I could get there."

Paulding ordered his men to load their pistols and wade ashore. He himself walked quickly to Lay. To

The death of Samuel Comstock.

South Sea islanders were ruled by kings. Here a chief is rowed by masked oarsmen.

make sure that Lay was not a mutineer, Paulding pointed his pistol at him and said, "Who are you?"

"I am your man," Lay said, and burst into tears.

"Tell the natives that if they rise from their seats or throw a stone we will shoot them all."

Lay shouted to the natives in their own tongue. Only one of them came forward—an old, wrinkled, white-haired man. He put his hand gently on Lay's arm. Paulding aimed his pistol at him, but Lay shook his head.

"Let me talk to him," Lay said. "He saved my life."

For a few minutes Lay and the old man spoke in low voices, while tears fell from their eyes. Then Lay waded out to the boat and, as the sailors rowed away, the old man stood in the surf, watching sadly.

Lay told Paulding that Cyrus Hussey was the only other member of the *Globe's* crew still alive. He took them to the small island on which Hussey was being kept. A few natives and their chief, Lugoma, were on the beach.

"He saved our lives once, too," Lay said.

But Paulding was taking no risks.

He held his pistol against Lugoma and said he would fire unless Hussey was turned over to him at once. The chief called out an order over his shoulder, and soon Hussey came walking up. Like Lay, he had been burned dark by the sun. He wore a small piece of blanket around his loins, and his blond hair, golden in the sunlight, hung down to his shoulders.

Paulding said to him, "Well, young man, do you wish to return to your country?"

His eyes filling with tears, Hussey answered, "Yes, sir. I know of nothing that I have done for which I should be afraid to go home."

Aboard the *Dolphin*, Lay and Hussey told their story. After the *Globe* had sailed away, Payne mistreated the natives. They attacked the white men, killing them with spears and clubs and stones. Lay, too, would have been killed if it had not been for an old couple who had taken a liking to him. They shielded him from the rocks with their bodies until the attack was over. Hussey was saved in much the same way. For twenty-two months the two Americans had lived with the natives. They had eaten with them, swum with them, fished with them, feasted with them. They had slept in grass huts, and watched the natives dancing to the thud of a big drum. They had seen the sun come up and the sun go down, the tides roll in and the tides roll out, and the days had passed like a boy's dream of summer.

In 1827, Lay and Hussey returned to their New England homes; Lay to Saybrook, Connecticut, Hussey to Nantucket. After a while on shore, they went whaling, and were never heard from again. Perhaps they went back to the islands. Perhaps, of all the men on the *Globe*, they were the only ones who truly found a kingdom—a peaceable kingdom in the unending summer of the South Seas.

A view of Valparaiso, Chile, where the escaped crewmen of the Globe *took their ship.*

SOUVENIRS OF WHALING

Six pictures of the whaler Charles W. Morgan. *'Tween Decks (above) with harpoons and other whaling implements.*

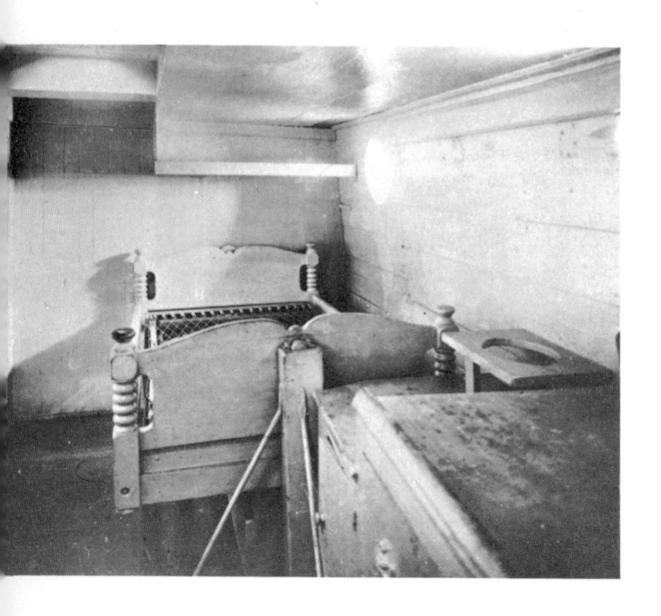

The captain's private stateroom (above) adjoins his comfortably furnished sitting room (below) in the vessel's stern.

After the schooner *John R. Manta* tied up at New Bedford in 1925, not a single Yankee whaler sailed the seas of the world. And when the old ships had rotted at the wharves, and the smell of whale oil had disappeared from the waterfront, what was left? Remnants, remainders, reminders . . . monuments and souvenirs of an industry that had once been great. There were the log books of forgotten vessels, the account books of merchants, the diaries, journals, and letters of whalemen and whaling wives. There were the curios brought home from the South Seas, scrimshaw, paintings and prints, some tools and utensils and weapons, bits and scraps of ships, and one complete ship, the *Charles W. Morgan.*

And then there were the stories, told by one person to another, or written down, of whales and whalers and whalemen, of all the living and dying that had made up the true history of whaling. Some of the stories were of real people and real happenings; others were like the tale of John Tabor's ride.

John Tabor was a whaleman who dearly loved a swig of rum. Once, on a voyage to the tropics, he went ashore. Standing on the beach, he saw a whale breaching not far off. At the same time, a long-haired old man came rowing up in a whaleboat.

"Get in, John Tabor!" the old man said. "Get in, and we'll catch that whale!"

John Tabor got in. The old man was a spry old man, and he harpooned the whale, leaped to its back and pulled John Tabor up after him.

"Hold fast, John Tabor!" the old man said. "Hold on like grim death!"

Taking hold of the harpoon, the old man sat astride the whale's back. John Tabor sat behind him, holding on to the seat of the old man's pants. And away they went, rushing over the ocean.

All night they rode, and in the morning they passed Nantucket. The old man still had a grip on the harpoon, and John Tabor still had a grip on the seat of the old man's pants. Turning north into Buzzard's Bay, the whale hit the beach at Taborstown at full speed. It slid across the sand and down Main Street, with men, women, children, and horses jumping out of the way, and

The forecastle, or crew's quarters, had narrow bunks. It was cramped, and crewmen's sea chests had to serve as seats.

The tiny galley (above) and the main cabin (below), where the captain and other ship's officers took their meals.

The Charles W. Morgan, *last of the old whalers, is preserved at The Marine Historical Association's Mystic Seaport in Mystic, Connecticut. Built at New Bedford in 1841, she saw 80 years of service. She sailed more miles and captured more whales than any other whaler, earning $2,000,000 for her owners. On her first voyage, lasting more than three years, she caught 61 whales, worth $69,591.*

"Gun ports" were painted on her hull to fool pirates. From 1887 to 1904, like a number of other Yankee whalers, she made San Francisco her home port and whaled in the Arctic. Her last voyage ended in 1921.

crashed into the town pump. The old man went flying through the air over the pump, leaving the seat of his pants in John Tabor's hands. John Tabor never saw him again, and shared the whale with his neighbors. It was a good-sized sperm and boiled down to about fifty barrels of oil. . . .

New Bedford had a favorite story called *The Whaling Classic*, which delighted many people, including Robert Louis Stevenson and Theodore Roosevelt. It was recorded in *The History of New Bedford* by Zephania W. Pease, as it would have been told by the mate of a whaler:

We was cruisin' down the Mozambique channel under reefed tops'ls, and the wind blowin' more'n half a gale, two years out er New Bedford an' no ile. An' the masthead lookout shouts, "Thar she blows!"

An' I goes aft.

"Cap'n Simmons," sez I (his bein' the same name as mine, but no kith or kin, thank God!), "the man at masthead sez 'Thar she blows!' Shall I lower?"

"Mr. Simmons," sez the cap'n, "it's blowin' a little too peart an' I don't see fittin' fer to lower."

An' I goes forrard.

An' the man at masthead sings out, "Thar she blows an' breaches!"

An' I goes aft.

"Cap'n Simmons," sez I, "the lookout at masthead sez, 'Thar she

1839.] '*Mocha Dick,' of the Pacific.*

MOCHA DICK:

OR THE WHITE WHALE OF THE PACIFIC: A LEAF FROM A MANUSCRIPT JOURNAL.

BY J. N. REYNOLDS, ESQ.

WE expected to find the island of Santa Maria still more remarkable for the luxuriance of its vegetation, than even the fertile soil of Mocha; and the disappointment arising from unexpected shortness of our stay at the latter place
the prospect of our remaining f
the former. Mocha lies upon

Before writing Moby Dick, *Melville read this true story about a white whale, in Knickerbocker Magazine, in 1839.*

blows an' breaches!' Shall I lower?"

"Mr. Simmons," sez the cap'n, "it's blowin' too peart an' I don't see fittin' for to lower."

An' I goes forrard.

An' the lookout at masthead sings out, "Thar she blows an' breaches, an' sparm at that!"

An' I goes aft.

"Cap'n Simmons," sez I, "the lookout sez, 'Thar she blows an' breaches, an' sparm at that!' Shall I lower?"

"Mr. Simmons," sez he, "it's blowin' too peart an' I don't see fittin' for to lower, but if so be you sees fittin' for to lower, Mr. Simmons, why lower an' be good an' damned to ye."

An' I lowers an' goes on the whale, an' when I comes within seventy-five foot of her I sez, "Put me jest three seas nearer, for I'm hell with the long harpoon." An' I darted the iron an' it tuk.

When I comes alongside the ship, Cap'n Simmons stands in the gangway. "Mr. Simmons," sez he, "you are the finest mate that ever sailed on this ship. Below, in the locker on the port side, there's rum an' seegars at your service."

"Cap'n Simmons," sez I, "I don't want your rum, no more your seegars. All I want of you, Cap'n Simmons, is plain seevility, an' that of the commonest, damnedest kind!"

An' I goes forrard. . . .

Greatest of all the whaling stories is Herman Melville's *Moby Dick*. A seaman in his early years, Melville made a whaling voyage on the *Acushnet*. During a gam, he met the son of Owen Chase, who had been the first mate on the *Essex*. Young Chase told him of his father's adventures on the ship that was attacked by a whale, and gave him a copy of a little book his father had written about it.

"I questioned him concerning his father's adventures," wrote Melville, "and when I left his ship to return . . . he handed me a complete copy of the *Narrative* [the book by Owen Chase]. . . . The reading of this wondrous story on the landless sea, and so close to the very latitude of the shipwreck, had a surprising effect upon me."

Some years later he heard tales of a ferocious white whale called "Mocha Dick." These tales, the story of the *Essex*, and what he himself knew of whaling churned through his mind. At last he sat down and wrote of the strange chase of a white whale that sent a ship and all its crew, except one, to the bottom of the sea. His book, *Moby Dick*, stands today as a monument to whaling.

There are other monuments, too, like the *Charles W. Morgan*, the last of the old whalers, preserved at the Marine Museum in Mystic, Connecticut. At New Bedford, under the roof of the Whaling Museum on Johnnycake Hill, is a half-size model of the whaler *Lagoda.* The original *Lagoda* was the favorite ship of Jonathan Bourne, a prominent whaling merchant. On one voyage alone she brought in a cargo worth $200,755. Bourne's daughter had the model built as a memorial to him. At both Mystic and New Bedford, and at the museums of Nantucket and Sag Harbor, are log books, scrimshaw, tools, weapons, utensils, paintings, prints, bits and scraps of ships, curios of the South Seas . . . souvenirs and monuments . . . remnants, remainders, reminders of the Yankee whalemen who sailed the far waters in the hunt for the most monstrous animal ever known on earth.

Whalemen never grew tired of telling the story of John Tabor's ride.

Sternboard of the bark Leonidas *of New Bedford.*

ACKNOWLEDGMENTS The editors are deeply grateful to Edouard A. Stackpole, curator of the Marine Historical Association at Mystic, Connecticut, for giving generously of his knowledge of Yankee whaling and for making available the museum collections and his personal collection; and to Philip F. Purrington, curator of the Old Dartmouth Historical Society and Whaling Museum in New Bedford, Massachusetts, for his advice and counsel, and for making possible the photographing of Benjamin Russell's panorama. In addition, they wish expressly to thank the following individuals and organizations for their generous assistance, and for their cooperation in furnishing pictorial materials from their collections: Chicago Historical Society—Miss Blanche Jantzen; Dukes County Historical Society, Edgartown. Mass.—Dr. Sidney N. Riggs; Mr. Chester Scott Howland, New Bedford, Mass.; Kendall Whaling Museum, Sharon, Mass.—Mr. and Mrs. Henry P. Kendall, Miss Jeanette Hurd; The Mariners Museum, Newport News, Va.—Mrs. Agnes Brabrand; Francis Russell Hart Nautical Museum, M.I.T., Boston, Mass.—Prof. Evers Burtner; Nantucket Historical Association—Mr. George W. Jones; Peabody Museum, Salem, Mass.—Mr. M. V. Brewington; Second Bank-State Street Trust Co., Boston, Mass.—Mr. Philip J. Potter, Mr. J. Bradley Scott, Jr.; Stonington Historical Society, Stonington, Conn.—Mr. T. G. Bradford.

PICTURE CREDITS

The source of each picture used in this book is listed below, by page. When two or more pictures appear on one page, they are separated by semi-colons. The following abbreviations are used:

CHS—Chicago Historical Society. All pictures from a journal kept by John F. Martin while on a voyage aboard the whale ship *Lucy Ann*, 1841–1844.

MIT—The Alan Forbes Collection, Francis Russell Hart Nautical Museum Department of Naval Architecture & Marine Engineering, Massachusetts Institute of Technology.

Mystic—Mystic Seaport, Marine Historical Association, Mystic, Connecticut. All photos by Louis S. Martels.

NYPL—New York Public Library.

Old Dartmouth—Old Dartmouth Historical Society and Whaling Museum, New Bedford, Massachusetts.

SST—Second Bank-State Street Trust Co., Boston, Massachusetts.

Cover "Capturing a Sperm Whale," an engraving by J. Hill; from a painting by William Page, based on a sketch, made in the 1830's by C. B. Hulsart—Kendall Whaling Museum, Sharon, Mass. **Front endsheet** "Peche du Cachalot," (Capturing the Sperm Whale), a lithograph by Martens, made in the 1850's after a painting by Garneray—Shelburne Museum, Shelburne, Vt. **5** Wooden figurehead from bow of whaler *White Lady*—Old Dartmouth. **6–7** "Peche de la Baleine," (Capturing the Baleen Whale), a lithograph by Martens, made in the 1850's, after an aquatint by Garneray—Shelburne Museum. **9** *Churchill's Voyages*, 1745, NYPL. **10** CHS. **11** (bot.) Mappemonde, 1546 by Desceliers, John Rylands Library, Manchester, England. **12** R. Morden, Map Division, NYPL. **13** (top) Drawn expressly for this book by Ray Pioch; (bot.) *Harper's Weekly*, Jan. 31, 1885, NYPL. **14–15** The Mariners Museum, Newport News, Va. **16–17** Small pictures—*Churchill's Voyages*, NYPL; Whale—Scammon, C. M., *Marine Mammals of the Northwest Coast*, American Museum of Natural History. **18** (top) New York State Historical Association, Cooperstown, N.Y.; (bot.) Old Dartmouth. **19** Old Dartmouth. **20** Whale—Scammon, *op. cit.*, American Museum of Natural History; (bot.) Barber, J. W., *Historical Collections of Massachusetts*, NYPL. **21** (bot.) Free Public Library, New Bedford, Mass. **22** (top) Old Dartmouth; (bot.) Mystic. **23** Logbook of Ship Wm. Baker, 1838, Old Dartmouth. **24–25** U.S. Fish Commission Report, 1875–76, NYPL. **26** (top) Collection of Rozelle Coleman Jones—Courtesy SST; (bot.) MIT—Courtesy SST. **27** MIT—Courtesy SST. **28–29** (all) Peabody Museum, Salem, Mass. **30–31** Collection of O. Kelley Anderson—Courtesy SST. **32** (top) *Harper's*, March 1861, NYPL; (bot.) Browne, J. Ross, *Etchings of a Whaling Cruise*, 1846, NYPL. **33** Browne, *op.*

cit. **34** (top) Browne, *op. cit.* **35** (top) Charcoal sketch by Clifford Ashley—Free Public Library, New Bedford. **34–35** (bot.) The Chase—Goodspeed's Book Shop, Boston. **36–37** (all) Mystic. **38–39** Panorama—Old Dartmouth. **40–41** Old Dartmouth. **42** (top) Scammon, *op. cit.*, Mystic; (middle) Old Dartmouth; (bot.) CHS. **43** Whaling Implements—CHS. **44–45** (all) Weir Journal—Mystic. **46** (top) CHS. **47** (top) Old Dartmouth. **46–47** (bot.) Panorama—Old Dartmouth. **48** Scammon, *op. cit.*, Mystic. **49** Chopping horse pieces—Browne, *op. cit.;* Mincing knife—Scammon, *op. cit.*, Mystic. **50–51** (top) Peabody Museum. **51** (bot.) Mystic. **52** Davis, William, *Nimrod of the Sea*, 1874, NYPL. **53** Scammon, *op. cit.*, Mystic. **54–55** Panorama—Old Dartmouth. **56** *Harper's*, June 1875, NYPL. **57** Phelps Stokes Collection, NYPL. **58–59** Panorama—Old Dartmouth. **61** (top) New York State Historical Association; (bot.) Old Dartmouth. **62** Map drawn expressly for this book by Ray Pioch. **63** (top) Old Dartmouth; (bot.) *Harper's*, June 1860, NYPL. **64–65** Panorama—Old Dartmouth. **66–67** Old Dartmouth. **68** (top) Old Dartmouth; (bot.) Collection of Mrs. H. Crowell Freeman. **69** Arthur Griffin, FPG. **70** Peabody Museum. **71** (both) Old Dartmouth. **72** (top) Courtesy Old Dartmouth; (bot.) Panorama—Old Dartmouth. **73** Kendall Whaling Museum. **74–75** (both) Panorama—Old Dartmouth. **76** (top) *Voyages of Captain Cook*, Mystic; (bot.) Browne, *op. cit.* **77** Cook's *Voyages*, Mystic. **78–79** Panorama—Old Dartmouth. **80** (both) Wilkes, Charles, *U.S. Exploring Expedition*, 1844, NYPL. **81** (top) Wilkes, *op. cit.;* (bot.) CHS. **82** Panorama—Old Dartmouth. **83** Panorama—Old Dartmouth. **84** Mystic. **85** Panorama—Old Dartmouth. **86** (top) *Tales of the Ocean*, Old Dartmouth; (bot.) *Harper's*, May 1874, NYPL. **87** The Mariners Museum. **88** Shelburne Museum. **89** (top) MIT—Courtesy SST. **90–91** U.S. Fish Commission Report, 1875–76, NYPL. **92** Old Dartmouth. **93** (both) Old Dartmouth. **94** Old Dartmouth. **95** (both) Mystic. **96** Mystic. **97** Cook's *Voyages*, Mystic. **98** Collection of Mrs. C. Richard Andrews— Courtesy SST. **99** (both) Old Dartmouth. **100–101** Letter—Nicholson Whaling Collection, Providence Public Library, Providence, R.I.; Portraits —Dukes County Historical Society, Edgartown, Mass. **102** (top) Shelburne Museum; (bot.) Mystic. **103** (both) Old Dartmouth. **104** (top) *Harper's*, June 1860, NYPL; (bot.) Weir Journal—Mystic. **105** (both) Mystic. **106–107** Old Lighthouse Museum, Stonington, Conn. **108–109** Stackpole, Edouard A., *The Sea Hunters.* **110** (top) *Magazine of American History*, 1880, NYPL. **110–111** (bot.) National Maritime Museum, London, England. **112** New-York Historical Society. **113** Mystic. **115** Collection of Mrs. Lovering Hathaway—Courtesy SST. **116–117** *Leslie's Illustrated Newspaper*, Jan. 11, 1862, NYPL. **117** (top) Meserve Collection. **118** (top) Nantucket Whaling Museum. **118–119** Panorama—Old Dartmouth. **120** *Harper's*, Aug. 1858, NYPL. **121** Panorama—Old Dartmouth. **123** Map drawn expressly for this book by Ray Pioch. **124–125** Panorama—Old Dartmouth. **126–127** Cook's *Voyages*, Mystic. **128–129** Panorama—Old Dartmouth. **130** Illus. by Rockwell Kent. Copyright 1930 & renewed 1957 by Rockwell Kent. From *Moby Dick* by Herman Melville. Reprinted by permission of Random House, Inc. **132** (top) Comstock, William, *Life of Samuel Comstock*, 1840, Boston Public Library; (bot.) Panorama—Old Dartmouth. **134–135** Panorama—Old Dartmouth. **136** Map drawn expressly for this book by Ray Pioch. **137** Comstock, *op. cit.* **138** Panorama—Old Dartmouth. **139** Browne, *op. cit.* **140–141** (all) Comstock, *op. cit.* **142** (top) Cook's *Voyages*, Mystic. **142–143** Kendall Whaling Museum. **144–145** (all) Mystic. **146–147** Dmitri Kessel, courtesy LIFE Magazine © 1958 Time, Inc. **148** *The Knickerbocker*, May 1839, NYPL. **149** Browne. *op. cit.* **150** Old Dartmouth. **Back Endsheet** "The Capture," a lithograph made in 1862 by Endicott & Co., N. Y., after drawings by A. Van Best and R. S. Gifford, corrected by Benjamin Russell—Goodspeed's, Boston. **Back Cover** (top left) The Whale Oil Man by Nicolino Calyo, The Museum of the City of New York; (bot. left) The Conflict, Shelburne Museum.

BIBLIOGRAPHY

The American Whaleman, by Paul Elmo Hohman (New York; Longmans Green, 1928)

The Boy Skipper Who Found a Continent, by William H. Kearns, Jr., and Beverley L. Britton (New York, American Heritage, June 1955)

The Bulletin, Old Dartmouth Historical Society and Whaling Museum, Philip F. Purrington, Curator (New Bedford, 1954, 1955, 1956, 1957, 1958, 1959)

The Charles W. Morgan, compiled by Marion Dickerman (Mystic, Connecticut; Marine Museum of the Marine Historical Association, 1949)

Follow the Whale, by Ivan Terrance Sanderson (Boston; Little Brown, 1956)

Ghost Ship of the Confederacy: The Story of the Alabama and Her Captain Raphael Semmes, by Edward Boykin (New York, Funk & Wagnalls Company, 1957)

The Great Story of Whales, by Georges Blond (Garden City, New York; Hanover House, 1955)

Historic Nantucket (Nantucket; Nantucket Historical Association, 1955)

The History of Nantucket, by Obed Macy (Boston, 1835)

The History of New Bedford, by Zephaniah W. Pease (New York; The Lewis Historical Publishing Company, 1918)

The Journal of Annie Holmes Ricketson on the Whaleship A. R. Tucker, edited by Philip F.

Purrington (New Bedford; Old Dartmouth Historical Society, 1958)

The Life of Samuel Comstock, the Terrible Whaleman, by William Comstock (Boston and New York, 1840)

The Loss of the Essex, by Edouard A. Stackpole (Nantucket; The Inquirer and Mirror, 1958)

The Maritime History of Massachusetts, by Samuel Eliot Morison (Boston; Houghton Mifflin, 1921)

Moby Dick, by Herman Melville

Mystic, the Story of a Small New England Seaport, by Carl Cutler (Mystic, Connecticut; the Marine Historical Association, 1951)

Nantucket Landfall, by Dorothy C. A. Blanchard (New York; Dodd, Mead, 1956)

Nantucket, the Far-Away Island, by William Oliver Stevens (New York; Dodd, Mead, 1936)

Nimrod of the Sea, or The American Whaleman, by William Morris Davis (Boston; Charles E. Lauriat, 1926; reprint of the 1874 edition, with an introduction by John R. Spears)

Polar Whaling, A Sea-Letter of a Cruise in the Okhotsk Sea in 1849, by William Henry Holmes (Mystic, Connecticut; Marine Historical Association, 1953)

Pictorial History of American Ships, by John & Alice Durant (New York; A. S. Barnes & Co., 1953)

Sag Harbor Express, Thursday, May 22, 1952; Vol. 91, No. 30

Sails and Whales, by Harry Allen Chippendale (Boston; Houghton Mifflin, 1951)

Scrimshaw at Mystic Seaport, by Edouard A. Stackpole (Mystic, Connecticut; Marine Historical Association, 1958)

The Sea Hunters, by Edouard A. Stackpole (Boston; Lippincott, 1953)

The Story of Old Nantucket, by William F. Macy (Boston; Houghton Mifflin, 1915)

Thar She Blows!, by Chester Scott Howland (New York; Wilfred Funk, 1951)

Two Dramatic Episodes of New England Whaling, by Sidney Withington (Mystic, Connecticut; The Marine Historical Association, 1958)

The Whale Fishery of New England (Boston; State Street Trust Co., 1915)

Whale Hunt, by Nelson Cole Haley (New York; Ives Washburn, 1948)

Whale Off! The Story of American Shore Whaling, by Everett J. Edwards and Jeanette Edwards Rattray (New York; Coward-McCann, 1956)

Whale Ships and Whaling, by George Francis Dow (Salem, Massachusetts; Marine Research Society, 1925)

Whale Ships and Whaling Scenes as Portrayed by Benjamin Russell, by Allen Forbes (Boston; Second Bank-State Street Trust Co., 1955)

Whaling and Fishing, by Charles Nordhoff (Cincinnati, 1856)

Whaling Wives, by Emma Mayhew Whiting and Henry Beetle Hough (Boston; Houghton Mifflin, 1953)

The Yankee Whaler, by Clifford W. Ashley (Garden City, New York; Halcyon House, 1942)

Yankee Whalers in the South Seas, by A. B. C. Whipple (New York; Doubleday, 1954)

FOR FURTHER READING

Young readers seeking further information on American whaling will find the following books to be both helpful and entertaining:

Cruise of the Cachalot, by Frank Bullen (New York; Dodd, Mead, 1947)

Dead Man's Gold, by Edouard A. Stackpole (New York; Ives Washburn, 1958)

Fast Iron, by Victor Mays (Boston; Houghton Mifflin, 1953)

The Great Story of Whales, by Georges Blond (Garden City, New York; Hanover House, 1955)

Harpooners, by Robert Ferguson (Philadelphia; University of Pennsylvania Press, 1936)

Moby Dick, by Herman Melville (New York; Random House, 1930)

Thar She Blows!, by Chester Scott Howland (New York; Wilfred Funk, 1951)

The Sea Hunters, by Edouard A. Stackpole (Boston; Lippincott, 1953)

Whale Hunt, by Nelson Cole Haley (New York; Ives Washburn, 1948)

Yankee Whalers in the South Seas, by A. B. C. Whipple (New York; Doubleday, 1954)

AMERICAN HERITAGE PUBLISHING CO., INC.

BOOK DIVISION

Richard M. Ketchum, *Editor*

JUNIOR LIBRARY

Ferdinand N. Monjo, *Editor*

Editorial Assistants

Judith S. Hozore • Malabar Schleiter

Judy Sheftel • Julia B. Potts

Mary Leverty

Designed by Jos. Trautwein

INDEX

Bold face indicates page on which illustration appears.